Canadian Aviation and the Avro Arrow

Fred Smye

Cover photo: Fred Smye's collection, Avro Aircraft negative 79406,
photographer Hugh Mackechnie

Copyright © 1985 Fred Smye

All rights reserved.

ISBN-10: 1500545996
ISBN-13: 978-1500545994

EPIGRAPH

Arrow Performance

Supersonic combat radius: 200 nautical miles.
Manoeuvrability of 2g at a speed of 1.5m at 50,000 ft. 5 mins combat.
   RCAF Specification

"With a radius of 300 nautical miles, a combat ceiling of 60,000 ft and a maximum speed at high altitude of 2m."
   Mr. Pearkes at the Defence Expenditure Committee, July 1960.

Radius and Range

Supersonic (1.5m) high altitude mission
   Supersonic combat (1.5m): 500 nm.
Long range mission subsonic (.92m)
   Supersonic combat (1.5m): 625 nm.
Ferry mission range: 1,500 nm.
   Official company data. Arrow 2A

"The subsonic radius of action is 506 nm. The radius for ferrying or for moving, in a non-combat state would be 750 nm.
   Mr. Pearkes at the Defence Expenditure Committee, July 1960

"[The Arrow] could not fly further than 150 or 200 miles at fighting speed."
   Mr. Diefenbaker on the CBC-TV program "Tenth Decade"

"The CF-105 would be able to do nothing but intercept and that within a very sophisticated ground environment and only within a range of 150 to 200 miles from its base."
   Diefenbaker Memoirs, Volume 3.

Costs and Prices Per Airplane

Diefenbaker's
Price for 100 operational airplanes: $12,500,000
   Diefenbaker statement September 23, 1958
Price for 100 operational airplanes
   with changed fire control system: $9,000,000
   Defence Expenditure Committee, July 1960

Pearkes'
> "If the alternative or modified fire control system had been introduced": $7,800,000

AVRO's
> Company version, using Government figures: $5,620,000
> Fixed price for 100 operational airplanes complete with fire control system: $3,500,000
> Estimated price of second 100 airplanes: $2,600,000

Termination

The Arrow and Iroquois "should be continued until next March when the situation will be reviewed again."
> Diefenbaker statement September 23, 1958

"What we decided last September was not to produce the Arrow under conditions which surrounded Arrow production at that time, but to re-examine the costs and then we will know where we are going."
> Pearkes, November 25, 1958

"We therefore decided to give what amounted to six months formal notice . . . in September . . . until March 1959 at which time we would make known our final decision."
> Diefenbaker Memoirs, Volume 3.

"Formal notice is being given now to the contractors."
> Diefenbaker, House of Commons, February 20, 1959.

"For that action the termination we gave notice of last September."
> Diefenbaker, House of Commons, February 23, 1959

FOREWARD

Fred T. Smye, once President and General Manager of Avro Aircraft Limited, first worked with the Canadian aircraft industry during World War II as an official of the Department of Munitions and Supply. In June 1940 he joined Munitions and Supply in the New York City office. Soon he became Executive Assistant to Ralph P. Bell, Director General Aircraft Production, Ottawa. Later Fred rose to Director of Aircraft Production and served as a member of the Aircraft Committee of the Joint U.S.- Canada Production Board. In 1944 he was appointed Assistant General Manager of Federal Aircraft Limited in Montreal to wind up the Canadian Government's aircraft production program.

At the close of the war he played a key role in establishing the British Hawker Siddeley Group in Canada through the formation of A.V. Roe Canada Limited. On August 1, 1945, Fred became the first employee of A.V. Roe Canada at Malton, Ontario; and with the official formation of Avro Aircraft on December 1, 1945, he was appointed Assistant General Manager. The new company took over the facilities of the war-time Crown company, Victory Aircraft at Malton to carry on research and development of jet aircraft to meet specific Canadian needs.

Fred Smye's friends and colleagues had always acknowledged his role as the driving force behind the administration of all the Avro projects: the Jetliner, the CF-100 the Orenda engines to power it, and the Arrow supersonic interceptor. As President of Avro Aircraft, he was largely responsible for the phenomenal growth and success of the company and its contribution to Canadian aviation—until the demise of Avro in 1959 upon the cancellation of the Arrow by the Diefenbaker government. This book sprang from 20 years of anger and frustration as Fred saw Canada ignore the Arrow achievement and forget a magnificent national story. But in the three or four years before he died in 1985, he had the satisfaction of seeing a new generation of Canadians re-discover the Arrow epic through publications, radio, and television.

Randy Smye
Oakville, Ontario.

CONTENTS

	Acknowledgments	i
1	Introduction	1
2	World War II and the Creation of a Canadian Aviation Industry	6
3	AVRO's First Ventures	22
4	The Arrow	51
5	Cancellation	70
6	Why? The Chaos That Followed	84
7	Retrospective	102

ACKNOWLEDGMENTS

Although many of the circumstances surrounding the cancellation of the Avro Arrow project in February 1959 were revealed finally in 1979 and 1980, some of my former colleagues think that I should add to the record as I was deeply involved in the whole affair. They also felt that I should publish the data which I have preserved over the 45 years since the beginning of World War II. I do so now in the hope that it will make some contribution to the history of the Arrow disaster and to Canadian aviation.

Without the persistent encouragement and assistance of my wife Linsey this story, even yet, would not be written. Encouragement and help also came from my good friends and former colleagues, Jim Floyd, the designer of the Jetliner and the Arrow, and Paul Dilworth, the original chief engineer of Orenda. I also wish to say thank you to Ken Church and Colin Johnson of the Orenda Company, and to Harry Keast, formerly of Orenda, who did the aerodynamics design of all the engines. I am also grateful to F.W. Hotson of De Havilland and Ian Geddes and Bill Joliffe of Canadair for providing data on their great companies.

Finally I must make reference to an excellent analysis of Canadian defence problems, done by an American scholar, Jon B. McLin, *Canada's Changing Defence Policy, 1957-1963* (Johns Hopkins Press, 1967). I have repeatedly referred to this fine document as a memory refresher and guide, for which I am grateful.

Fred Smye
Algarve, Portugal
1985

1

INTRODUCTION

In 1940 at the commencement of World War II, the aircraft industry in Canada consisted of eight companies turning out a handful of small aircraft in a combined shop area of some 500,000 square feet with a total employment of some 4,000 people. During the war the industry became Canada's largest, employing 100,000 people in about 6,500,000 square feet of floor area. A total of 16,418 aircraft were produced of which 5,874 were combat types.

Between the end of the war in 1945 and 1957 the aircraft industry became reconstituted, consisting of A.V. Roe Canada, Canadair and De Havilland, supported by a strong array of suppliers and subcontractors. During this period and for the first time, the design and manufacture of an aero engine was undertaken. It became known as the Orenda pure jet engine. A quantity of 3,838 were produced for installation in 690 CF-100's designed and produced by Avro and 1,025 F-86 Sabres produced under licence by Canadair. There were an additional 790 Sabres produced which were powered by a U.S. engine. The three prime contractors employed about 30,000 people. It was a strong and vigorous industry and probably the largest employer of engineers and technicians in Canada. The newly created companies of Avro Aircraft and Orenda Engines were engaged in the design and development of a supersonic fighter and its engine for the RCAF.

Likewise between the end of the war and 1957, the RCAF was reborn. It had nine squadrons of CF-100 and six squadrons of F-86 operating within the North American Air Defence Command as well as four squadrons of CF-100 and eight squadrons of F-86 operating in Europe within NATO. The RCAF was regarded as one of the great air forces in the Western Alliance.

The years 1957 and 1958 saw the election and the re-election of the

Diefenbaker government. In these years the supersonic Arrow was unveiled and had its first flight. During these years there was heated public debate over Canada's air defence policy and particularly over the development of the Arrow and its engine, the Iroquois. This raging controversy was climaxed by a press conference statement by Prime Minister Diefenbaker on September 23, 1958. This deliberately misleading, contrived political pronouncement contained obvious errors and contradictions. In my opinion, the most accurate description of it was provided by the late General Foulkes, then Chairman of the Joint Chiefs of Staff Committee. In a meeting I had with him shortly after the statement was issued, he referred to it as a "masterpiece of subterfuge".

In brief, the statement announced the procurement of the nuclear armed Bomarc-B anti-aircraft missile, the downgrading of the need, if any, for the manned interceptor, the installation of the Sage ground radar system, the cancellation of the Arrow fire control and missile systems to be replaced by others from the U.S., and an inflated cost of the Arrow on the basis of 100 aircraft which was contrived and without foundation. It also stated that arrangements were to be made with the U.S. government whereby the Canadian aircraft industry would act as sub-contractors to the U.S. industry. Finally it said that the Arrow and Iroquois projects would continue but would be subject to a review in March 1959 under conditions prevailing at that time.

Actually, the statement did not quieten the controversy and there were pundits in the media who were forecasting the certain death of the Arrow. They were right as, on February 20, 1959, the Prime Minister announced in the House of Commons, the immediate termination of all work on the aircraft and engine contracts thus throwing some 13,000 employees of the Malton plants on to the street. There was an estimated additional 10,000 workers discharged from the plants of sub-contractors and suppliers. The companies were also instructed to destroy the five supersonic airplanes which were flying, together with all the engines, all work in progress, all drawings, the vital engineering data, and in fact everything connected with the projects as if they had never existed.

On the grounds manufactured by Mr. Diefenbaker, the public seemed to accept his decision. There were those who thought that the highly skilled engineering teams at Malton should be preserved; but that consideration came a little late as the cream were on their way to the United States and elsewhere. At that time Mr. Diefenbaker was held in high esteem.

In August 1959, the Government announced that a contract was being placed with Canadair for the production, under licence, of 200 Lockheed F-104 aircraft for the RCAF. The primary armament was to be nuclear missiles. The airplanes were to fulfill a nuclear, strike attack role replacing the traditional defensive roles of the CF-100 and the F-86. This was a vital reversal of policy, the implications of which, in my opinion, were not understood by the Government at the time.

Two years after the manned interceptor was declared redundant by Mr. Diefenbaker, the Government announced that it had made arrangements with the U.S. government to acquire from it a quantity of 88 F-101-B interceptors. This somewhat obsolete aircraft was to be updated with air to air nuclear missiles.

At this time there was yet another defence controversy over the use of nuclear weapons. Mr. Diefenbaker had been evasive, as usual, as there was a strong division within his cabinet. The newly appointed Secretary of State for Foreign Affairs, Howard Greene, was vocally opposed to their use, but on the other hand the defence forces and particularly the RCAF were dependent on their use. Mainly due to his handling of the nuclear problem and in fact the whole matter of defence, Mr. Diefenbaker lost his majority in the House in the election of June 1962.

October 1962 was the month of the Cuban missile crisis. In it Canada was accused of not pulling her weight. It was obvious that the RCAF could not make much of a contribution but, moreover, the nuclear armed airplanes of the USAF were refused permission to operate over Canadian territory. In this highly charged atmosphere, Mr. Pearson, the leader of the opposition, who had also been sitting on the fence, pronounced that Canada should adopt the use of nuclear weapons so that she could live up to her commitments and obligations. In this regard, Mr. Pearson proposed a vote of no confidence in the House of Commons which was carried thus providing for the demise of the Diefenbaker Government.

A minority Pearson Government was elected in April 1963, but it was not for another year that the three main weapons systems of the RCAF became armed.

A major and debatable step by the Pearson Government was the unification of the armed forces. Arising out of this decision, 135 Northrop F-5 aircraft were ordered from Canadair. The F-5 is a light weight fighter bought to provide air support for the Army. As there really was no role for these airplanes, many of them were put in storage in an RCAF hangar in Trenton, Ontario.

In February 1969 an article appeared in the Toronto *Star* to commemorate the tenth anniversary of the death of the Arrow. Otherwise the debacle had generally been forgotten except, of course, for those who had been involved in the project.

The Trudeau Government revived the almost forgotten issue of air defence. The first act was to scrap the Bomarc missile stations. In 1972 it was announced that the aging Argus coastal patrol aircraft was to be replaced. Finally in June 1976 a contract was placed with Lockheed for 18 Aurora aircraft at a flyaway price of $38.7 million for delivery to commence in 1980. The major decision made in 1977 was to re-equip the RCAF with a fighter. The Minister of National Defence announced that a program had been planned at an estimated cost of $2.3 billion which should provide some 135 to 150 aircraft. Four U.S. companies and one European were asked to submit proposals for delivery to commence in 1981 for squadron use in 1983. In terms of performance, the Arrow was comparable to the aircraft under consideration but not as a weapons system due to the extensive development of fire control and armament systems. The Douglas-Northrop consortium was awarded the contract in 1980 for 138 F-18 aircraft at an estimated cost of $25 million each and an estimated program cost of $3.5 billion.

1979 marked the twentieth anniversary of the Arrow cancellation, but it was also the year of revelation of some of the facts involved in the Arrow affair. James Dow's book titled *The Arrow* was the best of three that were published on the subject. Dow's book was written on the basis of very extensive research and many interviews. It is professionally written without bias and tells most of the true story. In my opinion, he has cut through all the speculation, supposition, the smoke screens and red herrings in order to get to the heart of the matter. In a masterful manner, he spells out the Machiavellian ploys of Diefenbaker to destroy the Arrow, its engine, and the companies that built them.

"There never was an Arrow" was the title of an extensively researched CBC television documentary produced in 1979 but not aired until early in 1980. The title came from a comment made by one of those interviewed. In spite of the title, the program showed that there really was an Arrow, in fact, five of them flying at twice the speed of sound. It also showed a picture of them being cut to pieces with blow torches. It was an excellently produced, one hour program which painted the picture of the immensity of the disaster for Canada.

The aircraft industry as such, now consists of Canadair and De Havilland, both owned by the Government and both involved in uneconomic, commercial projects primarily for export at the immense expense of the Canadian taxpayer. Douglas Aircraft operating in the former Avro plant is acting as a sub-contractor to its parent company in the U.S. Canadian Pratt and Whitney is producing small turbines on behalf of its parent in the U.S. Spar Aerospace is successfully contributing to the U.S. space program. In essence, the industry is focused on the production of commercial products for export while, for its own defence, the country relies upon the supply of its military aircraft from the U.S.

To complete the circle and bring the episode up to date, reference should be made to the signing of an agreement by the President of the United States and the Prime Minister of Canada in March 1985 to install a "North Warning System". This advanced radar system is part of the defence against cruise missiles and nuclear armed bombers (declared obsolete 25 years ago). The cost is estimated to be U.S.$1.2 billion—of which Canada is to pay 40%. It is to be operational in 1992.

2

WORLD WAR II AND THE CREATION OF A CANADIAN AVIATION INDUSTRY

Pre-World War II

In 1939 Canada could scarcely have been considered an industrialized country. Rather, in the eyes of the world, Canada was looked upon as a far-flung, semi-polar region north of the United States noted for simple primary industries: farming, fishing, lumber, and mining. Although this assessment may have been harsh, it was not too far off the mark. The one truly modern industrial activity was automotive production which, in turn, had developed ancillary activities of steel production, metal forming, forgings, castings, and other related materials. But even the automotive industry could hardly be classified as indigenous, for the design engineering, production engineering, and top management were provided by parent companies in the United States. Perhaps more Canadian were the railway rolling stock and equipment industry, represented by Canadian Car & Foundry Company and National Steel Car Corporation, and the farm machinery and implement industry, represented by such companies as Massey-Harris and Cockshutt Plow. One industry under sudden development was aluminum, which was to make a major contribution to Canada's war effort.

To refer to Canada's pre-war aircraft industry would be an exaggeration of the term. Rather, it consisted mainly of skeleton structures to house a handful of machine tools, welding equipment, and the jigs and fixtures round which the airplane was wrapped. The group of companies comprising the industry employed 4,000-odd, occupied less than 500,000 square feet of space and produced about forty airplanes in a year. More particularly, the so-called industry consisted of the following:

- Boeing Aircraft Ltd., Vancouver, wholly owned subsidiary of Boeing, Seattle, producing Blackburn Sharks, a torpedo carrier for the RCAF. The quantity on order was fifteen.
- Canadian Car & Foundry Company, a builder of railway equipment with a vision of the future. In spite of immense obstacles it obtained an order from the RCAF for a few Grumman fighters. Correctly sizing up the situation, it went to the United Kingdom and, with some influential assistance, but great reluctance on the part of the British Government, gained an order for forty Hurricane airframes, skeletons as opposed to airplanes capable of flying. This company established its aircraft facility at Fort William.
- Canadian Vickers Ltd., Montreal a subsidiary of the British Vickers armament group. The plant was mainly for ship construction, but a portion was set aside for the assembly of a few Stranraer flying boats for the RCAF.
- De Havilland Aircraft of Canada Ltd., Toronto, a subsidiary of De Havilland, U.K. The Canadian company was a true pioneer in every sense of the word, sparked by its leader, Philip C. Garrett. The company was producing the famous Tiger Moth for the RCAF and for the odd flying club.
- Fairchild Aircraft Ltd., Montreal, a pioneer in bush flying airplanes, producing the U.S. Fairchild 71 and 82 for bush flying operators and the RCAF. Later, Fairchild also obtained a British order for Bolingbroke bombers, a Canadian version of the Bristol Blenheim.
- Fleet Aircraft Ltd., Fort Erie, a subsidiary of Fleet Aircraft of Buffalo, New York. The companies were named after their founder, Major Ruben Fleet, who moved the American company to San Diego and renamed it Consolidated Aircraft, which firm designed and built the PBY flying boat. The Canadian subsidiary was commencing to produce the Finch, a stick and string primary trainer for the RCAF.
- National Steel Car Corp., Malton, another producer of railway equipment with its plant located in Hamilton. Its president, Robert Mager, was a man of great vigour and imagination. He foresaw the future of the airplane and staked his right to a large piece of land adjacent to what was to become Toronto International Airport. He hastened to England and extracted from the British Government an order for twenty-eight Lysander army co-op airplanes. From this beginning would flourish the largest aircraft plant in Canada under the successive ownership of Victory Aircraft Ltd., A.V. Roe Canada Ltd., De Havilland, and ultimately and as of today, Douglas Aircraft of Canada Ltd.
- Noorduyn Aviation Ltd., Montreal, a small but bona fide aircraft

company in so far as its founder, Robert Noorduyn, was an aeronautical engineer and commenced the design of the Norseman, primarily for bush operation. It was, however, a good all-purpose airplane which later saw far-flung operations with the USAF.
- Ottawa Car and Aircraft Ltd., Ottawa, the last of the group, did no final assembly but acted as a sub-contractor to the others.
- As the result of a British Government mission to Canada in 1938, a company was formed under the name of Associated Aircraft Ltd. This company was to manage and coordinate production of the twin engine Hampden bomber by a consortium of Canadian Car, Vickers, Fairchild, Fleet, National Steel Car, and Ottawa Car. The assembly hangars were constructed for final assembly, one at National Steel Car at Malton and the other at St. Hubert airport, Montreal.

It must be remembered that in the pre-war era the airplane was far from being recognized as a means of transportation or as a major military weapon. Although the Canadian Government had formed Trans Canada Airlines in 1937 by merging a group of fledgling local carriers, nevertheless, it was generally believed that anyone using this mode of travel was a candidate for an asylum or the Victoria Cross. The RCAF was an air force in name only, as it had been reduced to a relatively small group of desk pilots through successive economy cuts by the Government. It was a rare event when, owing to some misadventure by the holder of the purse strings, a few gallons of gasoline became available to enable them to fly. This small band of fine men was dedicated to a belief and faith in the airplane and in flying. It was this group together with their civilian colleagues who formed the nucleus of the immense Joint Air Training Plan and the operational arm of the RCAF. Their associates in the industry, in spite of the odds, were no less dedicated and determined, thereby providing the foundation of what was to become Canada's largest wartime industry.

World War II

On October 10, 1939, the Prime Minister announced formation of the Joint Air Training Plan to be undertaken in Canada, in conjunction with the United Kingdom and the other Commonwealth countries, for training Commonwealth pilots and aircrew. Formal agreement for the Plan was signed in December 1939. The objective of the Plan was to produce 25,000 trained aircrew per year. The magnitude of this undertaking established Canada in the centre of the coming air age.

Under the terms of the Plan the U.K. was to supply the bulk of the aircraft, engines, and spare parts, the most important being the twin engine Avro Anson powered by Cheetah engines. Primary trainers, the De Havilland Moth and the Fleet Finch, were to be supplied from Canada. This provided a light aircraft requirement of the RCAF, in addition to which it had a need for operational aircraft in Canada. There was no requirement of the RCAF overseas as aircraft were to be provided by the RAF, under whose wing the RCAF would operate.

The spring of 1940 saw the collapse of France and creation of the Department of Munitions and Supply under the direction of The Honourable C.D. Howe, Minister. It was the responsibility of the Department to supply the needs of the Canadian armed forces and of the U.K. and Commonwealth forces in so far as they could be met in Canada.

Although the British endeavored to fulfil their commitment and, indeed, shipped a quantity of Ansons, it became evident that other and vigorous steps would have to be taken by Canada in order to prevent the collapse of the Air Training Plan. These steps were taken in two directions. One, to form a Government company to harness the Canadian industry to produce Ansons as quickly as possible. The second, to beg, borrow, or steal from the United States almost anything that would fly and which could serve as a substitute.

The Government company, Federal Aircraft Ltd., was formed immediately with headquarters in Montreal. Its first task was to re-engineer the airplane on the basis of engines, propellers, and equipment available from the US. Its second task was to farm out across the length and breadth of the country, the complete manufacture and assembly of the airplane. Federal established its own experimental shop in Montreal for the purpose of proving its re-engineering and substitute materials, of which there were many. It then named five final assembly contractors: Canadian Car in Amherst, De Havilland and National Steel Car in Toronto, Ottawa Car and MacDonald Bros. in Winnipeg. Additionally, hundreds of contracts were let for fabrication of components and parts.

A major problem faced by Federal was conversion from U.K. to U.S. standards. Drawings were different, as were material specifications, and each country had its own range of Standard Parts with different threads, etc. This problem was to haunt the Canadian industry throughout the war, as both British and American types were produced, overhauled, and repaired.

The first experimental Canadian Anson, designated Mark II, flew in January 1941. It was powered by Jacobs engines and Hoover propellers.

The first production Anson II with Jacobs engines flew in August 1941, and eighty-eight aircraft were delivered by the end of that year. This was a truly miraculous achievement. A total of 1,832 Anson II was produced.

The Mark II used a newly developed moulded plywood material to replace some aluminum parts. The improved Anson which became known as the Mark V incorporated a complete moulded plywood fuselage, many other improvements, and was powered by Pratt & Whitney engines. The first Mark V flew in January 1943 and a total of 1,050 of this type was produced, bringing the total Anson program to 2,882 airplanes produced at a peak rate of 100 per month. The Anson became the work horse of the Air Training Plan and was known as "The Flying Classroom" producing thousands of highly trained and skilled aircrew.

Parallel with the organization of the Anson program, additional and substantial orders were placed for the De Havilland Moth and the Fleet Finch. North American Aviation Company's Harvard, a single engine advanced trainer was ordered from the U.S. and arrangements made for its production at Noorduyn's plant in Montreal. Increased orders were also given Noorduyn for the Norseman. The British increased considerably their requirement of Hurricane airframes and of the Lysander.

At the same time, the RCAF declared its requirements for two operational aircraft, Consolidated Aircraft's PBY flying boat for coastal patrol to be purchased in the U.S., and the Martin B-26 bomber, to be produced under licence by National Steel Car at Malton.

All of the foregoing plans called for purchase of complete airplanes, engines, propellers, and a vast selection of parts and equipment in the U.S., without which the Air Training Plan would amount to naught. At this stage two important points should be emphasized. First, as with the so-called Canadian industry, the U.S. industry, in a relative sense, was also a fledgling. Wall Street would not recognize it as an industry, as such. The plants were relatively small and focused under the sunny skies of California. What gave the industry its great impetus was the placing before the war of huge contracts by the French and the British, particularly the latter. The contracts were for the Harvard advanced trainer, PBY flying boats, Lockheed Hudsons, Douglas DC-3s and Boston bombers, and P-51 Mustang fighters. They further contracted for all of the Pratt & Whitney and Wright engines and spares which their capacity would allow. A major British feat was an arrangement to have Packard Motor Company produce the Rolls Royce Merlin engine in Detroit.

As with their counterparts in Canada, the leaders of the U.S. industry were airmen, pioneers with an abundant faith in the airplane, but considered by the majority as being "far out". The industry was growing but far from the giant it was to become.

The second point was that the British, quite neatly but possibly quite rightly, arranged with the U.S. Government to act for all Commonwealth countries in the matter of war material required from the US. Accordingly, the only official Canadian Government contact with the U.S. Government would be by or through the British Government.

In order to administer their affairs in the U.S., the British and the French set up the Anglo-French Purchasing Board in New York. With the fall of France, the organization became the British Purchasing Commission under the chairmanship of Arthur Purvis.

It was into these circumstances that Mr. Howe and his newly appointed director general of aircraft production, R.P. Bell, ventured in the spring of 1940. The first item on the agenda was engines for the Ansons. As the capacity for Pratt & Whitney and Wright engines was sold out, the Canadians had to settle for the virtually unknown Jacobs engine, built by a small company of the same name in Pottstown, Pennsylvania. Similarly, all recognized airframe capacity was gone and, again, a small, little known company, Cessna Aircraft in Wichita, Kansas, was chosen to produce twin engine trainers, as insurance against and to supplement the Anson. These airplanes were also to be powered by Jacobs engines.

Further, contracts were let for PBY's and Harvards which were to be coordinated with British orders already placed and licenses negotiated for their manufacture in Canada. All U.S. contracts were negotiated and prepared by the British Purchasing Commission, but signed by the deputy minister in Ottawa. Canada was, after all, footing the bill.

By the end of 1940 a great deal had been accomplished. Procurement in the U.S. had been set in motion and channels of communication established. The Canadian aircraft industry scene appeared as follows:

- Boeing had completed its fifteen Sharks and was producing components for the Anson and Hampden.
- Canadian Car at Fort William was well into the ever increasing production of Hurricane airframes for shipment overseas. At its Amherst plant, assembly of the Anson was in progress as it was in the plant of Ottawa Car Company.
- De Havilland had production of the Moth well in hand, likewise, manufacture and assembly of the Anson.
- Fairchild was struggling with the Bolingbroke, as was Vickers with the handful of complex Stranraer flying boats, in addition to work on Anson components.
- Fleet was well along with production of the Finch and was producing components for others.
- National Steel Car was in production of the Lysander taken over by the RCAF upon the fall of France. Manufacture and assembly of the Anson was in hand. This firm was also preparing for production of the B-26.
- Noorduyn was increasing production of the Norseman and preparing for production of the Harvard.
- Associated Aircraft was beginning assembly of Hampden bombers in conjunction with and the support of Canadian Car, Vickers, Fleet, National Steel Car, and Ottawa Car.

This program of the industry left much to be desired. The British lost interest in the Bolingbroke, Hampden, and Lysander which were taken over by the RCAF to be used, in the main, as trainers. In any case, completion of production of these planes was in sight. The same was true of the Stranraer. This left the program with the following trainers: Anson, Harvard, Moth, and Finch, the utility Norseman, and Hurricane airframes for the RAF. It also left spare capacity which had been created since the outbreak of the war.

Plans and decisions made in 1941 provided the foundation upon which the aircraft program and industry developed into the nation's largest.

The magnitude and importance of British aircraft projects in the United States necessitated establishment early in the year of the British Aircraft Commission, located in Washington, the nucleus of which was the aircraft section of the former British Purchasing Commission in New York, now the British Supply Council. At the same time, the U.S. liaison office of the Canadian Department of Munitions and Supply was moved from New York to Washington. Although, officially, Canada could not deal with the U.S., unofficial contacts were made with senior officers of the War Production Board, the Army Air Corps, and the Navy Bureau of Aeronautics and a high degree of cooperation and coordination was achieved.

The U.S. Government, for its part, created the Joint Aircraft Committee, members of which consisted of the chief of the aircraft section of the War Production Board, the chief of staff of the Army Air Corps, the chief of the Navy Bureau of Aeronautics, and the head of the British Aircraft Commission. The function of this powerful Committee was to plan, schedule, and in fact, allocate the U.S. aircraft program on the basis of requirements channeled to it by the various agencies. The British represented the Commonwealth countries but, in due course, I was invited to join the Working Sub-Committee of the JAC, thus, becoming the first Canadian to be recognized by any of the wartime U.S. Government agencies.

The foreign exchange predicament in which Canada found itself was vastly eased by the Hyde Park Agreement, signed in April 1941. This enabled procurement agencies of the U.S., a neutral country already expanding its own war production, to buy war material from Canada. All purchases were to be channeled through a Canadian Government company, War Supplies Ltd., located in Washington. The officers of the various branches of the Department of Munitions and Supplies became salesmen for War Supplies Ltd. The first president of the company was E.P. Taylor. Difficult at the outset, the arrangement was accepted by the U.S. procurement agencies in time, and the representatives of War Supplies Ltd.

were recognized and dealt with in the same way as those of any U.S. company.

The first transaction of War Supplies Ltd. was negotiated with the U.S. Army Air Corps for Harvard and Tiger Moth aircraft and Link trainers. The procedure to conclude the transaction was involved but effective. The items were to be supplied by the British as their contribution to the Air Training Plan and, accordingly, a Lease-Lend requisition was placed with the U.S. Government. After wending its way through various Departments, the requisition arrived at the Army Air Corps procurement office at Dayton, Ohio, together with an authority to purchase. The recommended source was War Supplies Ltd. A contract was duly negotiated with War Supplies, providing for delivery to the British who handed them to the RCAF for use in the Air Training Plan. The paper work took this devious route, but the airplanes were produced in Canada and accepted by the RCAF on behalf of the United States and, in turn, the British.

With the implementation of the Hyde Park Agreement much closer cooperation and, in fact, integration was effected between the U.S. and Canadian production activities. Further, all dealings with the British were now conducted with the BAC. Thus, Washington became the focal point in all aircraft production matters.

The Hurricane Saga

Early in 1941 the U.K. Air Ministry cabled advice that no further Hurricane airframes would be required when present orders were completed. This meant that the big plant in Fort William employing some 8,000 would be out of work within about a year. It would take eighteen months to two years to put into production another aircraft. In the meantime there was a gap to be filled representing 400 airframes. Of what use would 400 airframes be to anyone? The only possible solution was to build them as complete airplanes. If this was practical, it raised the question of the supply of engines, propellers, and a full range of equipment. Further, if this could be accomplished, who wanted the airplanes? Not the RCAF who at about this time issued a requisition for 144 Bell Airacobras from the U.S.

The problem was put to the company whose chief engineer, Miss Elsie MacGill, said that the airplane could be re-engineered to take the Packard Merlin engine, the Hamilton Standard propeller, and a range of U.S. equipment and accessories. Even so, some few bits and pieces would still have to come from England.

As a result of preliminary discussions with British and U.S. authorities in Washington, sufficient encouragement was engendered to justify authorization by the Department of Munitions and Supply for the company to proceed with the re-engineering and production of 400 fully operational Hurricanes.

It was originally contemplated that the airplanes would be purchased by the U.S. Army Air Corps who agreed to allocate 240 of their Merlin engines and Hamilton Standard propellers, provided the British would do the same. This was more difficult for the latter as this vital equipment was urgently required in the U.K. With a little gentle persuasion by the U.S., however, the British finally agreed.

The Merlin 28 was to be produced for the British with drives to accommodate British accessories, whereas the Merlin V1650 for the Air Corps was to accommodate U.S. accessories. As neither of these engines would meet the new Canadian Hurricane requirement, a further type, the Merlin 29 was produced--the first engines from the Packard line.

Arrangements for the supply of the airplanes to China and/or the USSR were complicated, involving considerable delay. In the meantime, word was out that Canada had 400 fully operational airplanes, complete with guns and ammunition, for sale. The first customer was the Netherlands Government for service in the East Indies. It bought seventy-two airplanes for hard U.S. dollars aiding, thereby, Canada's foreign currency problem. As no other customer appeared on the scene at the time, it looked as though the Department of Munitions and Supply would have its own air force.

Pearl Harbour quickly changed the scenario. The Dutch requirement was eliminated and the RCAF commandeered the now famous 400, yet to be delivered. For the moment, apart from the PBY flying boats, there were no operational airplanes in Canada. The U.S. Government immediately imposed a ban on export of all war material in spite of which, however, with the cooperation of the chief of the Air Corps, ten Curtis Wright Kittyhawks were picked up by the RCAF pilots in civilian clothes from the plant in Buffalo, New York.

In the spring of 1942 an agreement was entered into by the U.S. and the U.K. to supply their ally, the USSR, with military aircraft. The U.S. were to supply bombers and the U.K. to contribute fighters. It became known as the Arnold, Portal, Towers Agreement after the names of the famed chiefs of the U.S. Air Corps, the RAF, and the U.S. Navy Bureau of Aeronautics, respectively.

With the passage of time, the Pearl Harbour crisis began to ebb and, under calmer circumstances, the Minister for Air, Charles G. Power, received a visit from Air Marshall Sir Christopher Courtney, representing the British Air Ministry. Amongst other things, he was after the Hurricanes which he received under Canadian Mutual Aid, gratis. The British, in turn, presented them to the USSR as their contribution under the Arnold, Portal, Towers Agreement. So, whereas the British and RCAF initially had rejected the Hurricanes, they both ended up with at least temporary custody of them in the involved chain of events leading to a contribution from Canada to the USSR. The RCAF requirement for the 144 Bell Airacobras also vanished and they, too, were taken over by the British to join the Hurricanes in the USSR, this time however at U.S. expense. Thus ends a complex saga of 400 Hurricanes and the RCAF Canadian fighter requirement in World War II.

The Mosquito

As the production of one great British fighter came to a close, another took its lofty place in the form of the Mosquito. This airplane was exceedingly versatile as was reflected in its many versions. It was used as a fighter and as a bomber and spearheaded the special target night raids when they would light up the target for the Lancasters. Many of its missions were unarmed.

The Mosquito was unique in that the fuselage was made of moulded plywood. The wings were wooden as were a great many other components and parts. In view of experience with the Anson V, it was believed that this would be an appropriate aircraft for production in Canada. The Mosquito was designed by De Havilland in England and the proposal for its manufacture in Canada came initially from De Havilland in Canada. An overly optimistic schedule of 115 per month was planned.

Increased demand from the RCAF and the British put the PBY into production at the Boeing plant in Vancouver and the Vickers plant in Montreal.

Similarly, because of RCAF, British and now U.S. Army Air Corps requirements, three versions of the Cornell trainer, PT-19A, PT-23, and PT-26, were put into production at Fleet, Fort Erie.

In the summer of 1941, Arthur Purvis, chairman of the British Supply Council, was killed in a trans-Atlantic air crash. He was succeeded by E.P. Taylor. Upon returning from his first visit to the U.K. in his new capacity, he informed a meeting in Washington attended by the Hon. C.D. Howe and R.P. Bell that his most important mission was to arrange for production of the Lancaster bomber in North America. As this was an impossibility as far as the U.S. was concerned, the challenge was thrown to Canada. It was accepted by Howe and Bell who undertook to produce thirty per month at National Steel Car, provided the British would guarantee the supply of B-26s for the RCAF from the US. Shortly thereafter preparations were being made at Malton for production of the famous Lancaster.

The RCAF B-26 requirement was subsequently changed to the Lockheed PV-21A patrol bomber which was ultimately delivered.

During the latter part of 1941, discussions took place with the U.S.

Army Air Corps concerning their interest in the Norseman. Serious discussions were also being undertaken with the U.S. Navy Bureau of Aeronautics with regard to the possibility of Canadian Car producing a dive bomber to follow the Hurricane and for increased production of PBY's at both Boeing and Vickers.

Pearl Harbour

When the U.S. joined the conflict in December 1941, plans under discussion with the U.S. Army Air Corps and the Bureau of Aeronautics for production of aircraft for their own requirements quickly became realities. The Navy entered into a major undertaking for production in Canada of its new, first line dive bomber, the Curtis Wright SB2C Helldiver. It was to be produced at Canadian Car, Fort William, at a rate of eighty per month. This became the project to follow the Hurricane. The SB2C Helldiver was also selected for production at Fairchild, Montreal, at forty per month to follow the Bolingbroke.

The PBY was basically a U.S. Navy airplane and, accordingly, this body requested an increased rate of production at Boeing and Vickers of twenty and thirty per month respectively. As part of this program, it was agreed that a large new plant should be built at Cartierville airport in Montreal to be operated by Vickers. Substantial expansion of the Boeing plant was also undertaken.

As there was a shortage of facilities in the U.S. for production of Hamilton Standard propellers, arrangements were made for the 12-D-40 to be made by a newly established subsidiary of United Aircraft U.S., Canadian Propellers Ltd., Montreal. A completely new plant was built for this purpose.

Although production of the Cornell trainer in Canada was arranged and under contract with the U.S. Army Air Corps, the types to be produced were for the British and the RCAF. After Pearl Harbour, production plans were substantially increased and a third type was added for use by the U.S. Army Air Corps.

At Noorduyn in Montreal, production of the Harvard was intensified and Norseman production was planned at twenty-four per month for the U.S. Army Air Corps.

A New Program

In early 1942, a new, vigorous and optimistic program was planned for the young aircraft industry. The types of trainers and combat airplanes to be produced were of the most advanced design. Their monthly rate of production and end user are listed in the following table:

SB2C	120	U.S. Navy
PBY	50	U.S. Navy, British, RCAF
Lancaster	30	British
Mosquito	115	British
Norseman	24	U.S. Army Air Corps
Harvard	80	U.S. Army Air Corps, British, RCAF
Cornell	150	U.S. Army Air Corps, British, RCAF
Anson	100	RCAF
TOTAL	669	

At January 1, 1942, 1,861 airplanes of the above types had been delivered. Additionally, 712 airplanes not contained in the program had been delivered for a total of 2,573.

This projected program with more advanced types of mainly all-metal aircraft dictated a considerable expansion of facilities, as well as purchase of machine tools and equipment from the U.S. A serious bottleneck occurred when it was discovered that much of this machine tool capacity was preempted by other munitions projects. The problem was overcome later in the year, however, by the "green light" directive issued by President Roosevelt giving aircraft requirements priority over all others.

The expanded program justified and in some cases necessitated Canadian production of ancillary equipment such as instruments. This program also required increased high precision forging and casting capacity as well as other materials made to exacting aircraft standards.

Heretofore, mention has been made only of prime contractors. Supporting these was a network of sub-contractors and suppliers who had to learn to work to aircraft tolerances and specifications. Massey-Harris in Toronto manufactured Mosquito wings. General Motors in Oshawa assembled complete Mosquito fuselages or, more accurately, endeavored to do so, as its continuing failures necessitated a third source, Central Aircraft Ltd. in London, Ontario. The Cockshutt Plow Company in Brantford built complete Lancaster undercarriages.

The aircraft program was not without its share of major problems. The Lancaster and Mosquito were of British design, to British specifications, using British equipment and accessories. It was, therefore, necessary to re-engineer both aircraft to accommodate U.S. materials and equipment. Some items, however, had still to come from the U.K. As indicated previously, the industry had to work to both U.K. and U.S. standards and specifications affecting every piece of equipment and raw material, even to the extent of nuts and bolts, including rivets.

The untimely death of Robert Magor, president of National Steel Car, resulted in a realignment of the top management of this company. This became unworkable, threatening the Lancaster project to such an extent that the Government expropriated the company's Malton plant.

A Government company was created in the name of Victory Aircraft Ltd., with J.P. Bickel as president. Subsequently, Mr. Bickel resigned over a difference in Government policy and was succeeded by V.W. Scully, who continued in that capacity until the end of the war and the takeover of the plant by A.V. Roe Canada Ltd.

David Boyd, manager of the Canadian Car plant in Fort William where he supervised the production of the Hurricanes, was brought to Malton as plant manager to spearhead the production of the Lancaster. In the reorganization, he became general manager of Victory Aircraft. Credit for the successful Lancaster project is mainly due to this dynamic man.

The De Havilland Mosquito project was too optimistic in its conception. This resulted in further problems, added to existing ones including management. It was one thing to build Tiger Moths, even to assemble Ansons. It was something else to produce a complex, first line fighter, using a novel wooden construction process. The Government had committed itself to schedules upon which RAF squadrons were being planned and progress at De Havilland repeatedly failed to materialize. Finally after much thought and with reluctance, the Government took over the company installing as controller, J. Grant Glassco, a former director. Although this action improved matters considerably, the project still suffered difficulties.

In addition to manufacturing problems, one of a technical nature arose, causing some aircraft to disappear without trace over the north Atlantic on ferry flights to the U.K. Owing to these losses, the RAF Ferry Command refused to accept any more airplanes. This position did not change after modifications were made to correct the suspected fault. Accordingly, a ferry flight operation was organized by John McDonough, president of Central Aircraft, London, Ontario, which continued until the end of the war without further loss.

Although the Mosquito project did not meet its vaunted expectations, nevertheless, a monthly rate of eighty-five aircraft was achieved and a total of 1,135 was delivered.

Achievement

At the outbreak of war, the aircraft industry consisted of eight small plants occupying some 500,000 square feet of space, employing approximately 4,000 people, and producing at an annual rate of about forty airplanes.

In 1944, the eight prime contractors occupied approximately 6,500,000 square feet of space in addition to great areas in use by sub-contractors and suppliers. The industry employed in excess of 100,000 people, the largest in Canada. Production stood at an annual rate of approximately 3,600 airplanes.

The varied nature of the types produced makes comparison of numbers of aircraft difficult. Weight of output is more realistic. The following provides a useful illustration:

	Aircraft	Weight
Last Quarter 1939	31	70,000 lbs
Last Quarter 1944	908	7,000,000 lbs

The wartime record of the industry

Combat Airplanes	5,874
Advanced Trainers	6,757
Primary Trainers	3,787
TOTAL	16,418

Value of production: $850,000,000
1944 Value of imports: 12.4%
1944 Value of exports: 78.6%

Although these statistics are a relative indication of achievement and performance, they cannot measure the extent to which the aircraft program enhanced Canada's industrial capacity. Manufacturing was carried out within exact tolerances and under controlled conditions previously unheard of.

New sub-industries were created for the supply of specialized equipment and materials broadening the base and know-how of industry in general, providing new skills and techniques. The production of an aero engine was considered to be too complex a task and, accordingly, was not undertaken.

It may be said that the Canadian aircraft industry made a substantial contribution to Canada's war effort and industrial capacity.

Towards the Future

During the war, Victory Aircraft converted eight Lancaster bombers to passenger carriers known as the Lancastrian. These airplanes were put into North Atlantic service in 1944 operated by Trans Canada Air Lines. This was Canada's entry into international airline service. The Lancastrians carried eight passengers plus some freight, consisting for the most part of mail for the forces overseas. This service provided invaluable experience for TCA and highlighted the necessity of a large, transport aircraft for post-war commercial operation.

In 1944 negotiations were entered into with Douglas Aircraft Company for a licence to produce in Canada a modified version of the DC-4. These negotiations resulted in the placing of a contract with Canadian Vickers, subsequently Canadair Ltd., Montreal, for DC-4 North Star aircraft powered by Rolls Royce Merlin engines. The contract was placed primarily on behalf of TCA but with the assumption that the aircraft would also be required by the RCAF.

In 1943, a small group of Canadian engineers was sent to the U.K. to learn about a revolutionary form of aircraft propulsion, the gas turbine jet engine. The engineers were granted free access to the very few plants working on an experimental basis in extreme secrecy.

The following year, the engineers returned to Canada to become the nucleus of a Government company being formed under the name of Turbo Research Ltd. The company was located in the plant of another wartime Government company, Research Enterprise Ltd., Toronto. Additional engineers were employed together with technicians, to advance their knowledge of this new form of aero power. Authority was granted to proceed with the design of an experimental engine.

Also in 1944, it was decided that the RCAF should put forth a requirement and appropriate preliminary funds to finance design study of a twin engine trainer as well as a jet fighter for its post war operations. This action was a reflection of Government policy to the effect that a post war air force would be maintained and would be supported by an industry capable of designing, as well as producing, airplanes to meet its particular requirements. The Government's policy was borne out of its wartime experience which established the following factors:

- The airplane had become the primary weapon in warfare and, accordingly, was of the highest priority in the future defence of Canada.
- The airplane had become a major factor in the field of transportation and would become increasingly more important in future.
- The air force should be reasonably independent and self sufficient within economic limits. It should not have to depend on others, as it did during the war, for its major equipment. The design and supply of its major equipment should be under its own control. It was emphasized, however, that its role would be purely defensive.

The advent of the jet engine placed the airplane in a role of immense future importance, the magnitude of which was difficult to comprehend.

In 1943, R.H. Dobson, managing director of A.V. Roe, Manchester, the designers of the Lancaster, and a director of the Hawker Siddeley Group, visited Canada to review Lancaster production at Malton, as well as the aircraft industry as a whole. He was impressed and formed the opinion that the post war activities of the Hawker Siddeley Group should be focused there. He further envisaged an industry complete with design and technical facilities. During this visit, preliminary discussions were held with the Government for the takeover of the management of Victory Aircraft. Nothing was concluded but ideas were planted for germination.

Two years later, in the spring of 1945, Dobson again visited Canada in an effort to enter into some form of arrangement for the takeover of Victory Aircraft. Although the war in Europe had just ended, that with Japan was still raging. Victory had some Lancasters to complete and was changing over production to the larger Lincoln, for operation in the Far East.

Dobson returned to England with a lease-purchase agreement for signature based upon the continued production of Lancasters and Lincolns. At the conclusion of the war with Japan in September, the Lancaster and Lincoln contracts were cancelled. Of the staff of some 9,000 at the Malton plant, all but about 400 were released.

3

AVRO'S FIRST VENTURES

A.V. Roe Canada Ltd.

With the end of the war, the aircraft industry including its suppliers virtually collapsed, the one exception being Canadair, preparing for the production of the North Star. Subsequently, De Havilland had some of its facilities returned, enabling it to begin again to design and produce what became its line of famous post war types.

Not only in Canada was it the case that the aircraft industry all but collapsed. The same was true in the U.S. and U.K. but, in those cases, the companies retained the nucleus of their management, engineering, and highly skilled staffs to undertake work in the post war era.

It was into this background that Dobson returned to Canada in November of 1945 with a signed agreement for the takeover of Victory Aircraft. The Government had assumed that he would back out of the agreement since its foundation, production of the Lancaster and Lincoln, had disappeared. This fact merely dictated an amendment to the agreement, whereupon it was signed. A.V. Roe Canada Ltd. was formed and took over the operations and facilities of Victory as of December 2, 1945.

Needless to say, the international aviation world, and most of his U.K. colleagues too, thought that this now famous man had lost his head. In their eyes this assessment was correct. Dobson's eyes, however, reflected a very different vision. He had unbounded faith in Canada, in Canadians, and in their future. He foresaw his young Canadian company with its vigour and enthusiasm leading the world in the limitless future of jet flight.

The name of the Canadian company was chosen by Dobson out of his immense pride in the renowned name of his own company, A.V. Roe Ltd., Manchester, a subsidiary of the Hawker Siddeley Group Ltd. This group was the largest and most versatile aircraft company in the world at the time. Notwithstanding the name, the Canadian company was wholly-owned, direct subsidiary of Hawker Siddeley.

A forceful director of Hawker Siddeley, Dobson's key colleagues were Sir Thomas Sopwith and Sir Frank Spriggs. From this group came the famous World War I Sopwith Camel and the Avro 504. The more recent claim to fame of the Group arose during World War II.

- A.V. Roe Ltd., designers and producers of the Lancaster and Lincoln bombers and, subsequently, of the Vulcan.
- Armstrong Siddeley Ltd., designers and producers of the Cheetah engine. A pioneer in gas turbine development, from which came the Sapphire engine.
- Gloster Aircraft Ltd., designers of the world's first experimental jet aircraft. From this beginning came the Meteor, the world's first operational jet.
- Hawker Aircraft Ltd., designers and producers of the famous Hurricane which played such a major part in the defence of Britain. Had it not been for the foresight and courage of this company, there would have been fewer of Churchill's famous "so few" in the Battle of Britain.
- High Duty Alloys, pioneers and producers of advanced technology forgings and castings, required by the rapid progress in aeronautical development.

Owing to British Government controls at the time, the parent company was unable to bring money from the U.K. The cost of incorporation of the company was met by J.P. Bickell, newly appointed chairman of the board. Initial operating expenses of the company were covered by a bank overdraft guaranteed in sterling by the parent company.

Walter P. Deisher, formerly VP and GM of Fleet Aircraft, was chosen as the VP and GM of the new company, replacing David Boyd. Mr. Deisher brought some key ex-Fleet personnel with him. Other than this change, the core of Victory Aircraft remained. It contained such stalwarts as Laurie Marchant, E.J. Solsby, Percy McQueen, Elwood Butler, Murray Willer, Henry Garside, Mario Pesando, Jack May, L.F. McCall, Ernie Alderton, Bob Johnson, Stan Wilson, Earle Brownridge, Don Rogers, Ron Adey, Bill Shaw and Joe Turner.

I was engaged by Sir Roy before the company's formation and was to be appointed Assistant GM. J.A. Morley and J.F. Taylor were also to join the company from the Department of Munitions and Supply. E.H. Atkin from A.V. Roe Manchester was appointed chief engineer, and he brought S.E. Harper with him as his administrative assistant. J.C. Floyd also came from A.V. Roe to head the civil aircraft engineering section and J. Frost from De Havilland was to head up military design. Jim Chamberlain, a Canadian with

Noorduyn Aviation in Montreal, was recruited at the outset as chief aerodynamist. In May of the following year the former Turbo Research team, led by P.B. Dilworth were to join the organization as the Gas Turbine Division.

This was the mixed group of some 400 odd, rattling around in an empty plant of some 1,000,000 sq ft, who were to undertake the design and production of a civil jet transport, a jet fighter and its engine.

The key people were for the most part relatively young—in their thirties. A.V. Roe Canada was a young company in every sense of the word. Their great asset was that they did not know that they should not be able to do what they did.

The Jetliner

Whilst Dobson, now Sir Roy, was visiting Canada, he had the opportunity of exploring the future needs of Trans Canada Airlines. One requirement which became evident was an inter-city replacement for the DC-3 and Lockheeds. This project was the first design study to be undertaken by the new engineering department, with a little assistance from "over 'ome".

The first proposal submitted by the company was for a four engine turbo-prop with a forty passenger capacity. This proposal was almost identical to what later became known as the Vickers Viscount, one of the main supporters and purchasers of which was TCA. The A.V. Roe proposal was rejected out of hand on the grounds that the proposed airplane must be a pure jet. This unalterable requirement was established as a result of a visit by Jim Bain, chief engineer of TCA to the Rolls Royce plant in the U.K. There, he saw the powerful Avon (6,500 lbs thrust) undergoing its early test bed running.

Although at first unconvinced, the company redrew the outline of the proposed airplane with two Avon engines. The projected performance was certainly revolutionary, if not sensational. A revised engineering and contractual proposal was submitted to TCA which resulted in a "letter of intent" to purchase thirty airplanes, provided they fulfilled the projected performance and price.

The specification called for a short to medium range jet transport with
1. A still air range of 1,200 miles;
2. A payload of 10,000 lb with seating for at least 30 passengers;
3. Cruising speed of at least 400 mph;
4. The ability to operate from 4,000 ft runways under I.S.A. conditions;
5. Approach and stalling speeds comparable with piston engine transports;

6. Operating costs comparable with existing transports;
7. Great stress was placed on reliability and maintainability to ensure operational reliability.

The estimated price was $350,000. This letter of April 1946, signed by H.J. Symington, president of TCA, set the wheels in motion for the company's first project under the technical direction of J.C. Floyd, who had arrived in Canada from the U.K. parent company in January of the same year.

To appreciate the significance and magnitude of this undertaking, one must remember the speed of current commercial aircraft: the DC-3, 135 mph, the DC-4, 200 mph. Even the latest fighters in service at the end of the war had not exceeded the speed at which this new passenger carrying aircraft was designed to cruise.

As indicated previously, in the latter part of the war, the RCAF initiated requirements for the Canadian design of an advanced twin engine trainer and a jet fighter. Both of these contracts were awarded to A.V. Roe in early 1946. As a result of more thorough examination between the RCAF and the company, it was not long before a decision was reached to drop or, in any event, to postpone the trainer project.

The question may arise as to why the contracts should have been placed with this new company. The explanation is that Victory Aircraft was, during the war, the largest and strongest aircraft company, particularly, in the engineering department. The cornerstone of A.V. Roe Canada policy was Canadian design and development, backed by vast engineering experience and facilities of the Hawker Siddeley Group in the U.K. No other Canadian company could provide this technical insurance. Further, it was the unstated policy of the Government to support two major aircraft companies. Canadair had the contract to produce North Stars and its policy was not one of Canadian design and development.

The jet fighter requirement was a long way from the detailed specification upon which design could proceed. Many months of discussion between the RCAF and the company ensued. Finally in late 1947, basic configuration was agreed upon and design commenced under the direction of John Frost, a recent arrival from the U.K. The airplane was to be known as the CF-100, a twin engine, long range, all weather, patrol interceptor with a crew of two. The engines were each to be of 6,500 lbs thrust.

Gas Turbine Division

As the Government's aircraft design projects were crystalizing, it turned its attention to the engine situation, more particularly, to the future of Turbo Research Ltd. The Government did not favour a continuation of crown companies into the post-war era. It was, therefore, looking for a sponsor to take over the operations, such as they were, of Turbo Research.

A basic Government stipulation was that any company taking over Turbo would make available to it, the technical data of the parent company. The Government favoured Rolls Royce or Pratt & Whitney, although the latter had very little jet engine experience at that time. In any event, the Government asked for proposals from these two companies, as well as from Bristol Aircraft in the U.K., and A.V. Roe Canada in conjunction with its sister company, Armstrong Siddeley, in the U.K.

Pratt & Whitney flatly declined, as did Rolls Royce with the comment, "the Canadians can build the Avon and stick a maple leaf on it if it will make them feel better". Bristol also declined on the basis of their opinion that Canada should not or could not produce, let alone design, a gas turbine. This left A.V. Roe Canada and Armstrong Siddeley, both members of the British Hawker Siddeley Group, who were keen and confident to undertake the job. In the meantime, Dobson had arranged with the British Government that all British gas turbine development data would be made available to the Canadian subsidiary through Armstrong Siddeley on a free exchange basis. Mainly, by default, A.V. Roe Canada was authorized to take over Turbo Research Ltd. and to carry on its work.

Almost all of the personnel of Turbo joined A.V. Roe and became established as the Gas Turbine Division. Ken Tupper, a senior engineer of the National Research Council and leader of the Canadian group in the U.K., chose to return to the NRC, but his valuable advice was always available. The chief engineer was P.B. Dilworth. His deputy and chief designer was Winnett Boyd. The chief development engineer was Doug Knowles. All were products of the University of Toronto. Wallace McBride the chief aerodynamist laid down such terms of employment that the company was unable to accept. Mr. Boyd flew to the U.K. to engage and return with a brilliant young aerodynamist, Harry Keast, a member of Sir Frank Whittle's team, who did an outstanding job on the aerodynamic design of the compressor and turbine blades in all of the company's jet engines.

Turbo had commenced preliminary design of an experimental engine of 2,600 lbs thrust, which was to become known as the Chinook, and work was authorized to be continued under a ceiling of expenditure and a deadline for test running. Behind this strict and austere approach, the Government was waiting to be convinced. In spite of the most makeshift conditions, the first engine ran, very successfully, on February 17, 1948.

It was under the deadline as to both time and cost. What was more important, it substantially met its specification in terms of thrust, fuel consumption, and weight.

With some reservation, but encouraged by progress on the Chinook, the Government authorized the start of design of a 6,500 lb engine, to become known as the Orenda. This was the engine to be required for the CF-100. It was the same thrust and general configuration as the Rolls Royce Avon, the most powerful engine ever to be conceived.

While the design, engineering, and technical phases of the company were taking shape, standing idle was a plant area of some one million square feet. In an effort to obviate this problem and to provide work for the shops, fifty-seven Lancasters were returned for storage and possible future use. As it happened, modification work on the Lancasters commenced almost immediately. Every one was put into useful service by the RCAF by the end of 1951 as versions for Air, Sea Rescue, Navigation, Photo Reconnaissance, and Long Range Patrol.

Also in the period 1947-1950 additional aircraft were overhauled and modified, mainly Venturas, Mitchells, and Sea Furies.

Jetliner Developments

Although design on the jet transport had commenced on authority of Mr. Symington's letter of April 1946, he believed that a transaction of this nature should be under direct jurisdiction of the Government, similar to that of the North Stars. On the eve of his resignation as president of TCA, he arranged for the Government to take over the contract. This new contract provided for a financial contribution of 75% by the Government and 25% by the company.

Mr. Symington was succeeded by Gordon McGregor, one of whose first pronouncements was that TCA would never buy and experiment with a new type until it had been proven by another airline. This put matters at cross purposes in so far as the aircraft was being designed primarily for his airline. He added that TCA personnel would be available to provide any assistance and advice that might be required. This problem was never resolved and did inestimable damage to the project. Other airlines undoubtedly questioned why Canada's own airline was not interested.

The next setback was the change of engines. Lord Hives, managing director of Rolls Royce, declared in the spring of 1947, that there would not be sufficient military experience with the Avon to justify civil use. As an interim, he suggested installation of four Rolls Royce Derwents which were the only jet engines with any military experience. But the Derwent was an older technology centrifugal flow engine with only half the thrust of the AJ 65 and higher fuel consumption, but there was no choice but to accept the only engine which appeared to be available.

The centre section of the aircraft had to be completely redesigned, but as the redesign progressed it became obvious that there were many advantages in the four-engined layout which allowed the landing gear to be tucked very neatly in the twin nacelles between the engines, resulting in probably the shortest and simplest undercarriage ever seen on any transport.

It would also have four engine reliability and easier control problems in the engine-cut case and better take-off performance in hot weather conditions. The nacelle arrangement finally designed would have made it much easier to fit better and more economical engines as these came along.

The four Derwent version would still have a good margin over the April 46 TCA specification to which the company was still committed.

The first flight of the Jetliner took place on August 10, 1949 for over one hour without incident. Although this flight followed that of the Comet by a matter of days, it was the first flight of a commercial jet in North America by several years. Canada had undisputed leadership in intercity air travel.

The second flight on August 16 was not so successful. During some intentional stall tests, the main undercarriage became locked in the up position with the nose gear down. The pilot elected to land the aircraft in that position which he did successfully with relatively little damage. The airplane was in the air again in a little over thirty days, September 20, when the flight test program began in earnest and continued without further incident. When Canada's own airline turned its back on "The Jetliner" as it was christened by the company, an all out effort was mounted to preach the gospel of jet transport to the leaders of U.S. airlines.

The features of the jet which are now taken for granted were considered as fantasy in those days. Such a pioneer as Captain Eddie Rickenbacker, president of Eastern Airlines, said, "Those jets are OK for the flyboys in the air force but you will never get paying passengers to fly in them". It was claimed that a jet could never operate in an air traffic control system. Jet thrust around an airport was out of the question, as it would burn up the tarmac and, probably, the air terminal itself. High fuel consumption was ridiculed without consideration of the fact that the price per gallon was one-third that of normal aviation gasoline. No consideration was given to the comfort and lack of vibration from the point of view of the passenger. Above all, the virtual doubling of speed was ignored as an economic factor. The sheer ignorance of the leaders and their experts was unbelievable.

At about this time, I accompanied Dobson on a trans Atlantic crossing in the fabulous liner, Queen Elizabeth. During cocktails in the skipper's cabin, the conversation turned to aviation. Dobson forecast to the skipper, that in the not too distant future, the mode of trans-Atlantic travel would be by jet aircraft, taking four to five hours rather than the present four to five days. The skipper found this observation hilarious, and he laughed and laughed.

In April 1950 the Jetliner was flown to New York at the invitation of Captain Rickenbacker on the occasion of the annual meeting of the Society of Automotive Engineers. The flight time was 59 minutes. It marked the first international flight of a commercial jet airplane, the first flight in the U.S., and the first carrying of mail by a jet transport.

Further demonstration flights took place in 1950 and 1951. In January 1951 a flight was undertaken from Toronto to Chicago to New York to Toronto. The flight times were Toronto-Chicago in one hour thirty minutes, Chicago-New York in one hour fifty-five minutes, and New York-Toronto in one hour ten minutes. Also in January 1951 the airplane was flown to Tampa, Florida, for test and demonstration flights returning from Tampa to New York in two hours twenty minutes. In the same month a flight was made to Winnipeg and return to Toronto with Ron Baker, chief pilot of TCA. Time to Winnipeg–two hours forty minutes, return flight–two hours thirty-five minutes.

Most of these flights were made at an altitude of 30,000 feet at speeds of 430 mph. When the pilot announced his altitude and ETA to ground air traffic control, it inevitably resulted in disbelief, if not near panic.

Today the flight times mentioned above are taken for granted. Not so in 1950-51, the age of the propeller driven DC-3 and DC-4, whose flight times were double those of the Jetliner. Records were established wherever the airplane flew and remained in force for at least seven years, until the advent of the 707 and DC-8.

An unbelievable fact was that few changes were required to the original design because of its sheer simplicity. Moreover, in 440 hours of flying, in all conditions, maintenance of this prototype airplane was negligible.

The following is a quotation from an article in the Fiftieth Anniversary issue of *Canadian Aviation* written by J.C. Floyd, designer of the Jetliner:

> The C-102 had been designed to the TCA requirement agreed in 1946, which called for a 36 seat aircraft with a cruising speed of 425 mph, a 'still-air' range of 1,200 miles, an average distance between stops of 250 miles, with 500 miles as the longest required. Allowances were specified as 45 minutes stacking, flight to a 120 mile alternate airport. Headwind was to be taken as 20 mph average with 40 mph maximum.
>
> The new theoretical TCA requirements called for a desired cruising speed of 500 mph, a 'still-air' range of 2,000 miles, distance between stops of 954 miles and headwinds up to 130 mph at 30,000 ft. Stacking was now to be up to two hours on some routes, etc, etc. As an indication of the severity of the new allowances, on the New York/Toronto run, the fuel needed for the actual flight of 364 miles was 9,400 lbs, but the reserve fuel to meet all of the new TCA requirements was 20,400 lbs making a total fuel load of almost 30,000 lbs on this short flight.
>
> It should be mentioned that these levels of allowances were never eventually used on any civil jet aircraft operated by TCA or anyone else, even on trans-Atlantic services.
>
> It might also be mentioned that, whilst TCA credited the Derwent engined Jetliner with only 300 miles range with thirty-six passengers using

their new fuel reserves, a much more detailed analysis carried out jointly by TWA and Avro engineers at Kansas City in April 1952 on precisely the same Derwent powered aircraft but using accepted TWA fuel allowances, resulted in a forty-passenger range of 940 miles.

Jetliner Specifications and Performance

	ORIGINAL TCA	DERWENT VERSION	NATIONAL AIRLINE	TWA MK.2
DATE	April 1946	1947-1950	1951	1952 (May)
ENGINES	2-AJ65	4-Derwent 5	4-Nene II	4-Nene II
THRUST SLS/ENG	6,500 lb x 2	3,600 lb x 4	5,000 x 4	5,000 x 4
GROSS WEIGHT	60,000 lb	60,000 lb	80,000 lb	89,000 lb
STILL AIR RANGE	1,200 miles	1,400 miles	1,900 miles	1,650 miles
PAYLOAD	10,000 lb	12,000 lb	12,000 lb	13,200 lb
SEATS	30+	40+	50	50-60
RANGE WITH FULL PAYLOAD	500 miles	500 miles	1,095 miles	1,200 miles
SPEED	400+ mph	427 mph	427 mph	450 mph
T.O. DISTANCE (ICAN)	4,000 ft	3,100 ft	4,750 ft	--
SOURCE	Agreed Spec April 1946	Paper to SAE January 1950	Section IV of C102 Report October 1950	TWA/Avro May, 1952

Gas Turbine Developments

A limited number of additional Chinooks were built for test and development purposes and, after considerable test bed running, proved the validity of the design. This provided confidence for the acceleration of the design of the Orenda.

In order to produce the necessary small quantity of test bed Orendas, some few new machine tools and equipment were acquired. Austerity was the order of the day, in spite of the fact that a relative handful of men were trying to produce this powerful engine–in an aircraft machine shop.

Notwithstanding the odds, the first Orenda ran ahead of schedule in February, 1949. Once again, to the amazement of everyone with the exception of the designers, the engine achieved its specified performance on its first series of runs. It was, in fact, the most powerful engine in the world.

During the development of the engine and, indeed, of the airplanes, a close liaison was maintained with senior officers of the U.S. Air Force. The chief of the material command, General E.M. Powers, resigned in 1948 to become president of one of the leading aero engine companies in the U.S., Curtis Wright Corp. of New Jersey. When he heard of the success of the Orenda, he was filled with disbelief. Invited to come and see for himself, he did so immediately. Upon his arrival at Malton the engine had logged an unbelievable running time in excess of one hundred hours. In the normal case of engine development, the engine is disassembled after several hours running for inspection. In the case of the Orenda, the very thorough instrumentation did not indicate the slightest cause of malfunction.

General Powers' inspection of the engine and its log books only heightened his disbelief. He asked that the engine be at least partly disassembled but the engineers refused. Only after an explanation of the considerable political implications did they reluctantly acquiesce. The engine was disassembled that night for the General's inspection the following morning. It was in near perfect condition and was immediately reassembled for an additional four hundred hours running to be terminated only by a personnel accident.

Not long after his visit, General Powers was due to return to sign a three part licensing agreement with the Canadian Government, Curtis Wright Corp., and A.V. Roe Canada. Such recognition by this pioneering engine company would have been of inestimable value to the Canadian firm. Early on the morning of the day of the proposed signing, there was a telephone call to say the General had become very ill in the night and could not attend. It was too late to inform Air Marshal Curtis who was on his way from Ottawa as the Government's representative.

While General Powers was convalescing, the chairman of Curtis Wright, Wall Street financier, Cornelius Shields, accompanied by senior engineers, set out for the U.K. to attend the SBAC show at Farnborough. During their visit, they were shown the Sapphire jet engine of Armstrong Siddeley, for which they signed a U.S. production license on the spot. That this jet engine should displace the Orenda by such a quirk of fate was a matter of great disappointment to the company, more especially since Curtis Wright were to encounter great difficulties with the British engine.

It should be pointed out that the U.S. was far behind Britain in development of jet engines. The leading U.S. engine manufacturers, Pratt & Whitney and Curtis Wright, worked to capacity in wartime producing piston engines, but had not had the opportunity to learn of the new form of propulsion. Further, development of the gas turbine was a closely guarded secret. Only General Electric, an industrial turbine constructor, ventured into the immediate post-war jet field and the maximum thrust attempted by them was the TG-190 of 5,000 - 5,500 lbs for installation in the F-86.

At Malton, however, throughout 1950, additional development engines were built and test bed running was accelerated towards a type test, the bench mark in aero engine development. Furthermore, the third CF-100, to be equipped with Orendas, was due to fly in mid-1951.

Although by a Herculean stretch of the imagination, one might consider the facilities adequate to build a handful of development engines, new and substantial quantities of machine tools and equipment were urgently required for the preproduction engines for installation in the CF-100s. Funding to purchase this equipment was eventually extracted from the Government, but no authority was granted to construct a proper engine plant. The new equipment, forming the preproduction shop, was to be laid out in the first aircraft assembly bay.

In the extraction process and upon being handed the letter of authority, I wished to ensure that the Minister, Mr. Howe, was fully aware of what was involved. On hearing the explanation, the Minister retrieved his letter, with the comment that many engines were designed and taken to a similar state of development but few produced. After assurance that the equipment could equally produce the Avon or the Sapphire, the Minister relented. In the process of the discussion I made a ten dollar wager with the Minister that the Orenda would be produced. At a much later date, the Minister, referred to the incident and the wager, in explaining the risk involved in aeronautical development, to the House of Commons. He neglected to say that he lost the wager and that he failed to pay.

During 1950, it was also decided to test the engine in flight. Two Orendas were installed in the outboard nacelles of a Lancaster which took off like a fighter. These tests proving successful, an Orenda was then installed in a U.S. built F-86 on loan by the USAF and, once more, the results were more than could have been hoped for. An A.V. Roe test pilot flew the airplane at 665 mph. Not long after, Jacqueline Cochrane, the world renowned American aviatrix, asked for an Orenda powered F-86 with which she broke five world's speed records for women.

Following agreement with the RCAF on configuration, design commenced in November, 1947. Two prototypes were to be built and tested before additional airplanes were ordered. These two were to be powered by the same Rolls Royce Avon engines at a reduced power of 6,000 lbs thrust. The first aircraft flew successfully in January, 1950, the second in July of that year.

The two-prototype restriction having been relaxed, an order was placed in May 1949 for ten preproduction Mk-2 aircraft powered with Orenda engines. The first of these flew successfully in July 1951. This first CF-100 equipped with Orendas was handed over to the RCAF by the Hon. C.D.

Howe at a ceremony at Malton. On that occasion, Mr. Howe said, "The aircraft as it stands before us is a notable achievement, marking as it does, a new milestone in Canada's industrial advancement." The remaining nine aircraft were delivered over the balance of the year, some in the form of dual control trainers.

In June of 1951 a production order was issued for seventy CF-100 Mk-3 airplanes. These, the first operational airplanes to be ordered in reasonable quantity, were to be powered with an improved Orenda Mk-2 engine also capable of installation in the F-86 Sabre. The CF-100 Mk-3 had a Hughes APG-33 radar system and a .50 gun package installed. The first of these airplanes was delivered in the spring of the following year. Once again, some of these airplanes were produced as dual control trainers.

As a result of test flying one of the preproduction airplanes in the fall of 1951, a buckled skin gave evidence of structural problems. A serious flap developed within the Government technical hierarchy. Accusations of technical integrity and threats of cancellation were hurled at the company. The chief engineer, E.H. Atkin, and I went immediately to England to confer with the best technical brains of the Hawker Siddeley Group. The reaction of the latter, when presented with the drawings illustrating the problem together with its proposed fix was disbelieving silence followed by great laughter. They were amazed at the necessity of a trans-Atlantic trip concerning such a routine, straightforward problem.

In order to reassure Canadian authorities, S.D. Davies, chief designer of A.V. Roe, Manchester, returned to Canada with us, whereupon the basic modification was incorporated in short order to everyone's satisfaction. We took advantage of Mr. Davies presence to have him investigate the stress condition of the design in general. His report was far from encouraging, resulting in major changes of personnel. Messrs Atkin and Frost were assigned to other duties and Mr. Floyd was persuaded to accept the position of chief engineer. He organized what became known as the Blitz Group under the direction of R.A. Lindley. This group, comprising some forty engineers and draughtsmen, redesigned the under stressed parts of the airplane on the shop floor as they were being made for the production of the CF-100 Mk-3.

Mr. Floyd was the father of the Jetliner the days of which were coming to a close temporarily at least, owing to pressure for the production of CF-100s and Orendas. In recognition of his work on the Jetliner, Mr. Floyd was awarded the Wright Brothers Medal, the first non-American to be so honoured. Offers of employment in senior capacities in the U.S. flooded his desk. The clear sensibilities of this fine man caused him to think of his first responsibility as being toward his own company, A.V. Roe Canada Ltd.

Mr. Floyd, as chief engineer assumed the ultimate technical responsibility throughout the continuing development of the CF-100. As vice-president, engineering, he assumed this same awesome responsibility for the Arrow. In complete dedication, he lead the teams which provided Canada with world leadership in aeronautical technology, only to be discarded by two successive Governments.

Korea

The war which started in Korea in mid-1950 gave the CF-100 and the Orenda a high degree of urgency. Until then development of the airplane and the engine were on a trial basis and, if successful, would go into service with the RCAF for the air defence of Canada. The Korean war eliminated theory in exchange for bona fide necessity. The year of transition was 1951.

The Jetliner project was put aside, in spite of the fact that negotiations were being finalized for the sale of ten airplanes to a major U.S. airline. The airplane continued flying, however, sometimes in conjunction with the CF-100 test programme.

Although a preproduction shop for the Orenda was being established in the first aircraft assembly bay, as previously mentioned, the decision was now made to construct a vast new engine facility. At the same time the decision had also been reached to install the Orenda in the F-86 Sabres to be produced by Canadair.

Although a production order of seventy CF-100s had been placed, it became evident that the quantity and configuration were inadequate, particularly with respect to radar and armament. Moreover, the continued successful development of the Orenda provided more power and efficiency.

These major and positive plans and decisions came to fruition in 1952. Machine tools were being transferred to the new engine plant early in the new year to supplement the large quantity of new, modern equipment which had been ordered. The plant, the most modern of its kind, was officially opened in September. The Orenda then commenced to be built on an efficient production line basis, the planned scheduled rate being one hundred per month.

Once again, the CF-100 was to undergo major design modification. In many respects it was becoming a different and far superior airplane. The most important change was brought about by a modification in armament which dictated a complete new nose section forward of the cockpit and a multitude of alterations to the cockpit and fuselage. This new armament consisted of the advanced radar and fire control system developed by the Hughes Aircraft Company, the MG-2 and rockets. Whereas the CF-100 Mk-3 had only a gun package which fired from the forward underside of the fuselage, the rockets were now added and fired from pods installed at the wing tips. A more powerful engine, the Orenda II of 7,300 lbs was also installed. This became the basic CF-100, the Mk-4. A contract for 330 airplanes was placed in early 1952 for production at thirty per month. The first aircraft was completed on schedule in September 1953.

Howard Hughes and the Jetliner

In the spring of 1952 representatives of the Hughes Aircraft Company came to Malton to discuss installation of their fire control system in the CF-100 Mk-4. One happy outcome of these discussions was an arrangement for Hughes to produce the front part of the nose structure in which the bulk of their equipment was to be installed. This they would ship to Malton complete, ready for reasonably easy connection to the main structure, thus immensely simplifying a complex task.

A different development, concerning the Jetliner arose out of these discussions. Howard Hughes was well known as a pioneer airman. He had vision, courage, ability, and 87% of the stock of TWA. It was suggested to him that he might consider the Jetliner for use by TWA, provided it could be produced in the U.S. under licence. The response from Mr. Hughes was immediate and, shortly, the airplane was on its way to California for his inspection.

The day following its arrival he had an extended flight and was impressed. During the aircraft's six months stay Mr. Hughes always took the controls. In this period, I had many meetings with him under, sometimes, unusual conditions. Although he had an office in which his communications centre was located, he was rarely there. Rather, he would operate from the Beverley Hills Hotel where he lived at that time, from one of his green Chevrolets, or from any number of locations which struck his fancy. There was no routine in his life; no difference between night and day. Hence, telephone calls at two AM or four AM. He slept when he was tired and ate when he was hungry. This made dealing with him a little out of the ordinary, frustrating usually, but never boring.

Other meetings were held between the chief engineers of TWA and A.V. Roe resulting in a modified version of the Jetliner acceptable to Mr. Hughes. The four Derwent engines were to be replaced by two Pratt & Whitney J-57 axial flow turbines, or four Rolls Royce Nenes. The parallel section of the fuselage was to be extended and additional fuel capacity provided. It looked a fine airplane to fly Chicago-Los Angeles.

A contract was entered into to provide for maintenance of the airplane while it was in the U.S. which also granted Hughes the rights for its manufacture in that country. Mr. Hughes made several attempts to arrange this and very nearly succeeded with Consolidated Aircraft, only to have the project rejected by the USAF due, again, to the pressures of the Korean War. Finally, Mr. Hughes pleaded with A.V. Roe to build thirty airplanes. This appeal the company was forced to reject after agonizing deliberation.

Much has been written about the mysterious Howard Hughes. He was certainly eccentric, a genius who operated a financial empire in his head. He was shy and wished privacy which he would go to any length to achieve. To A.V. Roe representatives he was always hospitable, courteous, and honourable.

The conclusion of the Hughes negotiations wrote the death warrant for the Jetliner, although it was flown occasionally until 1956 when it was dismantled.

The Jetliner belongs to aviation history. The Smithsonian Institution in Washington, interested in its preservation, finally declined. It was offered to the newly established aviation museum at Ottawa but was rejected, largely it was claimed, because of its size. All that remains are a few photographs which, even today, reflect a magnificently designed and proportioned airplane, and the sad but glorious memories of those who designed, built, and flew in it.

What a different story it might have been had four Jetliners been built immediately following the prototype and handed to TCA for experimental flying on selected routes, say, New York-Toronto-Montreal. In due course, passenger service could have commenced using the Derwent engines until an axial flow engine was ready for commercial service. Valuable experience would have been gained by A.V. Roe and TCA out of which could have grown the first commercial jet service in the world. A.V. Roe Canada was the only company in the world with combined jet aircraft and engine experience and facilities upon which TCA was free to draw. The Jetliner could have been the DC-3 replacement. There need never have been British built Viscounts operated by TCA. The airlines of the world would have beat a path to Malton.

Orenda, Sabre, CF-100 Sales

By mid-1953 the first Orenda powered Sabre was delivered–the fighter with the highest performance in the Western world. Early the following year, the 1,000th engine was produced and the first Orenda powered Sabres were on their way to the RCAF in Europe.

In 1955 the CF-100 Mk-5 was introduced with an increased wing span and yet more powerful engines to increase altitude performance. By the end of that year more than 400 CF-100s had been delivered.

January 1957 saw the first of four squadrons of CF-100s transferred to RCAF 1 Air Division in Europe.

For many months negotiations were in progress with the Government and air force of Belgium for purchase of CF-100s. Competition was British, French, and American. The major snag for the CF-100 proposal was release of the MG-2 system by the U.S. on security grounds. Funds for the purchase of the aircraft were to be provided through U.S. Mutual Aid. Once the security problem of the MG-2 had been overcome and choice was unrestricted, the CF-100 was selected. The announcement of the sale of fifty-three airplanes was made in June 1957.

A significant aspect of this transaction was the fact that it was accomplished only with the assistance of Donald Quarles, Secretary of the USAF. He was instrumental in overcoming the security problem and in making the Mutual Aid funds available despite keen competition for the contract by the American Northrop F-89. It might also be added that the sale was made in spite of the Canadian Government, more particularly, certain air force officers. Subsequently, however, both the Government and the RCAF contributed magnificently to ensure successful operation of the airplanes by the Belgians.

It is also significant that in 1957 a NATO partner should choose the CF-100 all weather fighter for the air defence of its country in the light of the statement by a Canadian prime minister, approximately one year later, that there was no need for a supersonic interceptor for the air defence of his country.

A further version of the CF-100, the Mk-6 providing higher altitude with Orenda Mk-12 engines and missile armament capabilities, was all but completely engineered when it was summarily cancelled by the incoming Diefenbaker Government in the fall of 1957.

The Mk-5 was therefore the last version of the CF-100 production of which was concluded in December 1958.

CF-100 Production Summary

Mark 1 prototype	2
Mark 2 preproduction	10
Mark 3 production	70
Mark 4 production	330
Mark 5 production	280
TOTAL	692
Belgian Air Force	53

Orenda Engine Production Summary

Series 1 development engine	10
Series 2 development engine	22
Preproduction engine	50
Production for F-86 Sabre	1,723
Production for CF-100	2,023
TOTAL	3,838

In operation and maintained in Canada, West Germany, South Africa, and Colombia.

Aircraft Data

Jetliner

	TCA	TWA
Engines:	4 Derwent	4 Nene II
Cruise speed mph:	427	450
Still air range (miles):	1,400	1,600
Range with full pay load:	500	1,200
Gross weight (lbs):	60,000	83,000
Passengers:	40	50-60

CF-100

Radius of action: 15 minutes combat at 689 nautical miles
Operating altitude: 45,000 ft
Operating maximum speed: Mach .88
Operating maximum dive speed: Mach 1.03
Maximum gross weight : 36,000 lbs

CF-100 and Orenda Summary

At the start of the aircraft and engine programs at Malton, a lack existed in engineering and manufacturing experience as well as in facilities for components and accessories. Initially, these were supplied from the U.K. and the U.S. It was, however, a condition of the experimental contracts that both design and manufacture be established in Canada as soon as volume warranted.

With regard to the Orenda, the entire fuel and combustion system was supplied by Joseph Lucas in the U.K. This was a vital component of the engine and Lucas was the sole source of supply. Patented alloy and large, complex, compressor casing castings were supplied by High Duty Alloy, a sister company in the Hawker Siddeley Group in the U.K. Steel turbine blades were supplied from the Steel Improvement Company of Cleveland. Precision gears came from various U.S. sources. Additionally, sources were located in Canada for the development of new materials and manufacturing techniques some of which, at the outset, were considered by the suppliers to be ridiculous.

An unexpected problem became apparent a few short months before the first engine was to run. There was no jet fuel, JP-1, i.e. kerosene, available to run the engine. The Canadian petroleum industry was not particularly interested in getting into the business at the time, but one company did so, to a limited degree, as a gesture to the Government and to A.V. Roe.

In the case of the CF-100, undercarriage wheels, tires, and brakes originally came from Dowty Equipment Ltd. and Dunlops in the U.K.

Dowty also supplied pumps and valves. Plessey, U.K., supplied pumps and electrical equipment. Godfrey Associates, U.K., supplied pressurization equipment. Ejection seats for the airplane came from Martin Baker of the U.K. Initially, nearly all instrumentation came from either the U.K. or the U.S.

The volume of items emanating from the U.K., including engines, was great enough to warrant a company representative in London to coordinate and ensure supply.

With the establishment of the Canadian programs, engineering and manufacture of all ancillary equipment was increasingly located in Canada. From 1953 onward, virtually the entire CF-100 and Orenda were produced in Canada supported by appropriate technology. A complete self-contained aircraft and aero engine industry had been created.

This growth of advanced technology not only served the CF-100 and Orenda projects, but formed a foundation which developed and spread to enhance Canadian industry generally.

Costs and Prices

Aircraft costs and prices provide variations without end which tend to confuse the uninitiated. As with most statistics, these may be presented in a form to justify the position being advanced.

Normally, and as in the case of the CF-100, the cost or price of the airplane is the work carried out by the aircraft producer, including the installation and testing of the engines and fire control system supplied by the Government.

The costs or prices of the 680 production CF-100s were as follows:

Mark 3	70	$690,142 each
Mark 4	330	$416,970 each
Mark 4 and 5	280	$376,590 each

To these figures must be added sales tax of 10% which is passed from one Government Department to another. To achieve the cost of the complete aircraft, prices for the engine and fire control system must also be added, thus—

	330 x Mk-4	280 x Mk-4 & 5
Aircraft	$416,970	$376,590
Sales Tax	41,697	37,659
Engines (2)	120,000	100,000
Fire Control	53,000	53,000
TOTAL	$631,667	$567,249

Tooling for the production of the aircraft is contracted for separately and is usually considered separately. These costs are not now available but, as a rough estimate, could be in the order of $15,000,000 or a cost of approximately $22,000 per aircraft.

Similarly the cost of the basic design, test, and development, is contracted for separately and may or may not be added to the cost of the quantity produced. It would be wrong to add the total cost of this expenditure, since a great deal of the work is an advance in the state of the art and applicable to aircraft design and technology generally. Again, it might be estimated that this cost, applicable to the CF-100 would be in the order of $15,000,000.

When aircraft are delivered to the RCAF, they require maintenance. This, in turn, requires spare parts for the complete airplane, including the engine and fire control system. Special ground handling equipment must be provided, also, elaborate fully illustrated handbooks and manuals. It has always been the practice to charge these expenses to the RCAF maintenance account, where they belong.

At various stages of the CF-100 and Orenda projects there was criticism of the cost plus contracts. There may have been some justification in the early stages because of the expansion of the organization, the small quantities ordered, and the constant changes required. With the stabilizing of production of the Mk-4 as well as of the quantity to be produced, however, the company submitted a target price proposal. This the Government was reluctant to accept as its senior officers thought it to be unreasonably low. Following persuasion, the proposed price for 330 aircraft was accepted. The profit was such on both the aircraft and engine contracts that large amounts of undue profit were voluntarily repaid to the Government.

The Government and the RCAF, with comparable data available to them, have repeatedly stated that they paid less for the CF-100 than would have been the case for a similar but inferior airplane from the U.S.

In terms of cost and economics, there can be no doubt of the success of the CF-100/Orenda program. Close to the entire investment remained within the Canadian economy as against total procurement outside the country. Thousands of engineers, skilled and semi-skilled workers were trained and developed, thus strengthening Canada's industrial base. A major step was taken in the advancement of technology. Not the least of the benefits was the value of the export.

A.V. Roe Canada Ltd. Organization

A.V. Roe Canada Ltd. was incorporated in December 1945, taking over the facilities of Victory Aircraft Ltd. at Malton. In May 1946 A.V. Roe also took over the operations of Turbo Research Ltd. There were separate aircraft and engine divisions of the company, but each used common functions wherever practical.

The original directors and officers of the company were:
J.P. Bickell: Chairman
R.H. Dobson: President
Sir Thomas Sopwith: Director
Sir Frank Spriggs: Director
J.S.D. Tory: Director
Walter Deisher: Vice President and General Manager
Fred T. Smye: Assistant General Manager

In the fall of 1951 a major change in management was undertaken upon the resignation of Mr. Deisher. Crawford Gordon became president, Fred Smye became executive vice president, and Sir Roy Dobson became chairman, replacing the late J.P. Bickell.

Under this management, aircraft and engine divisions became all but self-contained. In addition to their corporate functions, Smye became acting manager of the aircraft division and Gordon for the engine division. Gordon did not remain in this capacity for long, as he arranged with General Motors for the loan of Thomas McRae, a senior engineer of the Allison Engine Division. In due course Smye became general manager of the aircraft division and W.R. McLachlan was to be appointed to a similar capacity in the engine division succeeding McRae.

The two divisions became completely separate and fully incorporated companies with Mr. Gordon as president of both in December 1954. Messrs Smye and McLachlan became vice presidents and general managers of Avro Aircraft Ltd. and Orenda Engines Ltd., respectively. At about the same time Canadian Steel Improvement Ltd. was acquired from the Steel Improvement Company of Cleveland, Ohio. These three companies were wholly owned subsidiaries of A.V. Roe Canada Ltd. which, in turn, became the holding company.

Shortly before the tenth anniversary of A.V. Roe Canada Ltd. in 1955, the company acquired Canadian Car & Foundry Company which was celebrating its fiftieth birthday. Canadian Car's rail car and bus production was flourishing, as was its foundry for production of huge commercial castings. It was also producing the T-34 Mentor for the RCAF.

The following year the foundry division of Canadian Car became a separate company, Canadian Steel Foundries (1956) Ltd. It was a wholly owned subsidiary of A.V. Roe Canada Ltd. The former manager of the foundry division, Gordon McMillan, became president. In August of that year A.C. MacDonald joined the company as vice president of Canadian Car, becoming president in June 1957.

In 1956 Smye and McLachlan were appointed presidents of Avro Aircraft and Orenda Engines, respectively.

As A.V. Roe Canada was not now wholly dependent on defence work, it was believed that the public should be given the opportunity to participate in this Canadian enterprise. In the fall of 1956, therefore, it became a public company by issuing shares, with Hawker Siddeley retaining the majority and control.

A significant year in the development and further expansion of the company followed in 1957. Canadian Applied Research was acquired. This company was engaged in the development and production of aerial photographic and navigational equipment as well as in base electronic and instrumentation.

A major acquisition was the controlling interest of Dominion Steel and Coal Corp (Disco). This company was mining iron ore in Newfoundland and coal in the Maritimes. It operated a basic steel plant in Sydney, N.S., and a shipyard in Halifax. The company had steel fabricating plants in Montreal and Toronto. It was a large, basic Canadian firm.

With this further expansion, adjustments were made in the senior management of the company. F.T. Smye was appointed executive vice president, aeronautical, of A.V. Roe Canada, responsible for all aeronautical activities of the company and chief executive and president of the following, listed together with the respective vice president and general manager.

Avro Aircraft Ltd., A/V/M J.L. Plant
Orenda Engines Ltd., E.K. Brownridge
Canadian Applied Research, J.M. Bridgman
Canadian Steel Improvement, J. Wellings

A.C. MacDonald was appointed executive vice president, industrial, of the parent company responsible for the company's industrial activities carried out by the following, listed together with the respective president:

Canadian Car & Foundry Company, S.G. Harwood
Dominion Steel and Coal Corp, Crawford Gordon
Canadian Steel Castings Ltd., G.L. McMillin
Canadian General Transit Ltd. 55%, C.H. Drury
Canadian Steel Wheel Ltd. 50%, G.L. McMillin

W.R. McLachlan was appointed executive vice president, administration, of the parent company responsible for all head office staff functions.

The board of directors of A.V. Roe Canada at that time and until 1959 was as follows:

Sir Roy Dobson, Chairman
Crawford Gordon, President
Fred T. Smye, Executive vice president
A.C. MacDonald, Executive vice president
W.R. McLachlan, Executive vice president
Sir Thomas Sopwith
J.S.D. Tory
W.P. Scott

Avro's First Ventures

Colin W. Webster

At the end of 1957, A.V. Roe had become one of the largest and most diversified companies in Canada employing some 25,000 people. Its operations extended virtually from coast to coast. It was a producing company engaged in mining raw materials, forging and casting materials to serve manufacturing industries, producing basic steel products and materials, fabricating finished and semi-finished products, producing rail, sea and bus transport products, carrying out advanced aeronautical technology, and producing the most advanced aircraft and engines. The pride of the organization, the result of twelve years endeavour, had just been unveiled to the world–the Arrow.

As in every undertaking, it is people who count. From its meagre beginning in December 1945, when the staff numbered some 400, it rose to 4,000 at December 1950. This was the period of experimentation and preproduction. From December 1950 to December 1952 the increase was 11,000 to a peak of 15,000. The extraordinary build up in employment was sparked by the war in Korea and the immediate necessity for planning and construction of facilities as well as for the series production of both the CF-100 and its engine.

Every conceivable type of engineering personnel was urgently required. The case was similar in technical aspects of tooling and production. Skilled workers in almost every trade were required in large numbers. New skills had to be learned for the operation of new machine tools and equipment created for manufacture of the gas turbine engine. The reservoir in Canada from which this vast range of personnel could be drawn was virtually dry.

To solve this problem, a large scale immigration program was undertaken in conjunction with the Federal and Ontario Governments. Employment offices were opened in England. Transport and housing accommodation in Canada had to be provided. This employment scheme was a major undertaking in itself. Thousands of workers were involved and, in the majority of cases, their families as well.

The immense influx of employees had to be indoctrinated and trained in varying degrees and skills. Some of this training was carried out on the job but a great deal was done in a large company school created and staffed for this purpose.

This major immigration project of skilled and semi-skilled workers together with the output from the company school also made a significant contribution to Canada's industrial strength.

The extent and complexity of the services and facilities of a company such as Avro is probably not widely appreciated. The Avro facilities were in operation twenty-four hours a day, seven days a week but greatly reduced in scale on Sunday. Until the early 1950s the company had its own water system, supplied by its own wells, some miles away. It also supplied water to the village of Malton and the Toronto airport. The company operated its own extensive sewage disposal system.

As the projects were secret, a large security force was necessary, involving a staff similar to a small city. A modern fully equipped fire department was maintained, not only for protection of the vast plant but also to be on hand for test flights. A relatively small but modern hospital was operated twenty-four hours a day, with a resident doctor and a staff of nurses.

The company had a large, fully equipped cafeteria and two separate dining rooms. Providing a food service for some 5,000 to 6,000 people is no small chore. The operation of the facilities was sub-contracted to professional caterers.

There was a large photographic department engaged in every aspect of photography and photographic reproduction. Likewise a large printing facility. Voluminous, fully illustrated publications are necessary for the airplane and all of its equipment. The publications department was made up of some 125 illustrators, artists, and technical writers; even so, some of this secret work had to be sub-contracted.

Similar facilities and services were provided at the Orenda Engine Company.

The Canadair Connection

Canadair was incorporated in 1944 taking over the former aircraft division of Canadian Vickers, located at Cartierville. Its first major project was during World War II when 369 Canso (PBY-5) flying boats were produced for the U.S., U.K., and Canada.

In 1947, Canadair was purchased by the Electric Boat Company of Groton, Connecticut, to form the nucleus of what was to become General Dynamics Corp in 1952. Oliver West, a former senior officer of Boeing, Seattle, was appointed president of Canadair.

The first post-war project of the company was the production of a modified version of the Douglas DC-4 fitted with Rolls Royce Merlin engines, the North Star. This airplane was developed for TCA but was also sold to CPA, BOAC, and the RCAF. Air travellers of the time may recall that this airplane was somewhat noisy which gave rise to controversy, culminating in a row in the House of Commons. There were seventy-one produced.

In August 1949 Canadair received the go-ahead for the re-engineering of the North American Aviation F-86, to meet the requirements of the RCAF. The first aircraft was completed in November 1950. The first 790 aircraft had the U.S. produced General Electric J-47 engine installed. Of the total of this type produced, 292 were for the RCAF, 60 for the USAF and 438 for

Avro's First Ventures

NATO and the RAF.

The next version of the F-86 had the Orenda series 10 engine installed. There were 370 of this version produced for the RCAF. The final version of the F-86 had the more powerful Orenda series 14 engine installed, of which a quantity of 655 was produced. Deliveries of this type were made to the following countries: Canada, (RCAF): 390; West Germany: 225; South Africa: 34; Colombia: 6; TOTAL: 655

Of the total of 1,815 of all types produced, 1,052 were delivered to the RCAF for operation in Canada and Number 1 Air Division in Europe and 763 were for export. The approximate value of these export orders was $234,000,000. The rate of production varied, but the planned, and achieved, peak rate was two per day.

Within its time scale of the early and mid-fifties, the Orenda powered Sabre, as it was called, was the highest performance interceptor in the world. It would fly rings around its U.S. counterpart at NATO exercises. The last airplane was delivered in October 1958.

Almost concurrent with the F-86, the company produced a modified Lockheed T-33 trainer with a Rolls Royce engine installed. The go-ahead for this program was given in July 1951. The first aircraft was completed in December 1952 and production proceeded at a peak rate of about thirty per month. All of the aircraft were for delivery to the RCAF. The program was successfully completed in March 1959 after a total production of 652.

Also in the early fifties, Canadair undertook the production of thirty-three Argus aircraft to fulfil the long range patrol requirement of the RCAF. The Argus was, again, a modified version of an existing type, namely, the Bristol Britannia. These airplanes are still in service, as of 1979.

A follow-on program of, basically, the same aircraft but with a "swing tail" the Yukon, provided the RCAF with twelve transports. An additional twenty-seven of the airplanes were exported to commercial operators.

In the closing days of Mr. Diefenbaker's regime, his Government placed a contract with Canadair for 190 CL-41 jet trainers which the company had signed. The first aircraft was produced in December 1963 and production was planned for a peak of ten per month. Malaysia bought twenty of these airplanes, the production of which was completed in October 1967. The airplane was powered by a General Electric J-85 engine which was produced by Orenda.

In early 1966, Canadair started production of the CL-215, a multi-purpose amphibian, which the company also had signed. The aircraft was capable of carrying a 12,000 lb pay load and of operating out of small water areas as well as from semi-prepared strips. One of its main applications was as a fire fighter. It had been ordered in relatively small quantities by the province of Quebec, France, Spain and Greece.

Canadair had other major projects which will be covered in later chapters.

De Havilland Aircraft of Canada

Shortly after the war, the Downsview plant was returned to De Havilland under the management of P.C. Garret. The first project was construction of fifty DH-83C, a Canadianized version of the pre-war Fox Moth. The company's first design project was the Chipmunk Trainer of which 217 were built in Canada. Because of the excellence of the design and an urgent requirement, 1,000 Chipmunks were produced by the parent company in the U.K. A further quantity of sixty Chipmunks was produced in Portugal.

The second De Havilland project was more ambitious. It was the design and development of a relatively small general purpose single engine transport with short takeoff and landing characteristics. This basic design concept became the DH trademark with world wide recognition. The first type in this successful line was christened the Beaver. The first flight took place in August 1947. There was a total of 1,632 produced and sold throughout the western world. The U.S. Army became interested in the concept of the Beaver and bought 981 of a military version. This marked the beginning of a close association between the U.S. Army and the company.

Following the success of the Beaver, the company maintained the same design concept, but with twice the capacity and pay load, to produce the Otter. The first flight took place in December 1951. There was a total of 466 Otters produced and amongst many customers were the U.S. Army, the U.S. Navy, and the RCAF.

While carrying on with production of the Beaver and the Otter, the company undertook production of one hundred Grumman CS2F-1 Tracker carrier based, anti-submarine aircraft for the Canadian Navy. The first Tracker rolled off the production line in August 1956.

With the successful experience of the Beaver and Otter behind them, the company undertook design of a super Otter of 28,500 lbs equipped with two Pratt & Whitney R-2000 engines of 1,450 hp. This airplane was named the Caribou and first took to the air in July 1958. There was 307 of this type produced and, once again, 190 were delivered to the U.S. Army in a military version.

The availability of the PT-6 turboprop engine from Canadian Pratt & Whitney enabled the Beaver to be re-engineered to take the lighter and more efficient engine. The first aircraft flew in December 1963 and a quantity of sixty was produced. It was named the Turbo Beaver.

Similar philosophy with regard to the new turbo power plant was applied to the Caribou which was also re-engineered and became known as the Buffalo. It first flew in April 1964.

The next type was the Twin Otter designed initially to take turbo engines. At the time of writing, there were some 500 airplanes produced since first flight in May 1965. The Twin Otter filled a need for feeder airline operators in the U.S. and elsewhere, as well as for the military. It is being operated in fifty-four countries.

Throughout its post-war history, De Havilland stayed with a line of practical, efficient airplanes to meet particular needs of commercial operators and the military. Each successive type grew bigger and better but retained the characteristics of versatility and ability to operate in and out of short runways. De Havilland is a recognized world leader in STOL aircraft engineering.

The latest and current project of the company is the four engine commercial airliner, the DASH 7. Again, it is designed around the same philosophy: to meet a particular need, practical efficient, and in and out of short runways, quietly.

The plant occupied an area of, approximately, 110,000 sq ft and peak employment reached almost 5,000.

De Havilland Aircraft of Canada Ltd., owned by the Hawker Siddeley Group Ltd. of the U.K., was sold to the Government in 1974 for a price of about $40 million.

Canadair Ltd., owned by General Dynamics Corporation of the U.S., was sold to the Government in 1976 for a similar amount.

The main project of De Havilland is the DASH 7, a short range civil airplane with a restricted market in Canada. The future of the project and possibly the company will depend upon its ability to sell in the export market.

Canadair's main project is the CHALLENGER which is the most sophisticated of the business jets. It is twin-engined, high speed, relatively long range and incorporates the latest technology. The airplane was designed in the U.S. and the drawings, technical data, etc. were acquired by Canadair for production in Canada. Once again, this is a civil airplane with a very restricted market in Canada, and consequently its future will also depend on the highly competitive export field.

The Government will have a lot of money invested in these civil projects, the risky success of which will depend exclusively on markets outside Canada. This appears to me to present a peculiar set of circumstances and an unusual function for the Canadian Government, particularly when it is required to go outside the country to meet its own defence requirements. The arrangements seem to be a little back to front.

Aircraft Production Summary 1950-1958

Operational
Canadair: F-86, Sabre 1,815; Argus--45
De Havilland: CS2F-1 Tracker--100
Avro: CF-100--692
TOTAL: 2,652

Trainers
Canadair: T-33--652
De Havilland: Chipmunk--217
TOTAL: 869

Commercial and Other
Canadair: Yukon--27
De Havilland : Beaver--1,632; Otter--466; Caribou--307
TOTAL: 2,432

GRAND TOTAL all types: 5,953

Jet Engines: 3,838

In Summary: the post WW II Canadian Aviation Industry

Important conclusions were reached out of experience gained during World War II:
- That the airplane had become a predominate factor in defence and in transport;
- That, with respect to Canada, air defence was to receive priority over other aspects of defence;
- That, within reasonable economic limits Canada would strive for the maximum degree of independence in her own defence;
- That there would be the closest possible coordination and cooperation between the United States and Canada in all matters of defence, particularly, the air defence of North America.

European countries were weakened by the conflict, whereas Canada had gained industrial strength and experience. During the war Canada had demonstrated her industrial and military capabilities and had won for herself a prominent place in the community of nations.

Canada played an important role in the formation of the United Nations. Canada made a major contribution to the organization of NATO and was recognized as an important and active partner. Through these activities, a close relationship was developed with other major powers, particularly, with the U.S. When the Korean War erupted in 1950, Canada was in a state of reasonable preparedness and made her contribution along with U.S. forces and industry.

Canada demonstrated willingness to assume increased responsibilities by making a major contribution to joint defence, particularly in the air. The RCAF became a major force in western defence with eight F-86 and four CF-100 squadrons operating in NATO. In conjunction with the U.S. Air Force, the RCAF had six squadrons of F-86 and nine squadrons of CF-100 operating in the air defence of North America. The CF-100 squadrons were located at St. Hubert, Uplands North Bay, Comox and Bagotville. The RCAF carried out its responsibilities for the coastal patrol of its area with long range Argus aircraft. The RCAF had an inventory of some 1,200 modern operational airplanes. In conjunction with the USAF, a vast network of radar ground installations was conceived and put into operation to provide an early warning system against attack from the air. The RCAF was reborn as an important, independent force under the outstanding and inspired leadership of Air Marshal Curtis. Out of his wartime experience he learned of the necessity of having its vital equipment within its own control. This philosophy was perpetuated by his successor, Air Marshal Slemon.

It would not be possible to record the development of the post-war aircraft industry in Canada without reference to Air Marshal W.A. Curtis, CAS of the RCAF from September 1947 to January 1953. Amongst his wartime assignments he was a senior officer attached to RCAF overseas headquarters in London. In that capacity he was involved in the allocation of aircraft and supplies by the U.K. Air Ministry. He could not always obtain the equipment which in his opinion was required by the RCAF squadrons. For example, although Six Group, Bomber Command, was wholly Canadian and some of their Lancasters produced at Malton, aircraft, spares, etc. had to be requisitioned from the British Air Ministry. His wartime experience in having the RCAF dependent upon others led to his dedication to independence for the Canadian Air Force in future.

In his capacity as chief of the air staff, he fought for and gained this independence. He was responsible for the rebirth of the RCAF, as well as for establishing it in its place of supremacy in the defence forces. He enjoyed the confidence of the Cabinet Defence Committee which supported him in the development of the RCAF into one of the great air forces in the western world.

Upon his retirement from the RCAF and in spite of more financially rewarding opportunities he joined the board of directors of A.V. Roe Canada Ltd. It was his belief that in this way he might best continue to serve the interests of the air force.

Canada also demonstrated industrial technological capacity in the design, re-engineering, and production of advanced aircraft and engines. Canadian produced airplanes were in the service of the air forces of Canada, the U.S., in NATO, and in South Africa.

Canada was well represented in matters of external affairs, defence, and industry by Louis St. Laurent, C.D. Howe, Lester Pearson, Brooke Claxton, and Ralph Campney. These men were highly regarded in the councils of the western world. When they spoke they were listened to and their opinions respected. They spoke from a foundation of industrial and military strength and as representatives of a country with a limitless future.

In order to formalize and strengthen North American air defence, the Governments of the U.S. and Canada agreed to establish the North American Defence Command (NORAD) with headquarters at Colorado Springs. The commander was to be an American, General Pertridge, and the deputy a Canadian, Air Marshal Slemon, who had retired as chief of staff of the RCAF for this purpose. Although the NORAD agreement was worked out by the Liberal Government, it was formally signed by the incoming minority Conservative Government of J.G. Diefenbaker in 1957. Unfortunately, this was accompanied by an unnecessary hubbub in the House of Commons, the first of a long succession, which, apparently quite unjustly, sowed the seeds of mistrust by the new Government of its military advisers.

4

THE ARROW

Design

In July 1953 a design study contract was awarded to Avro to enable design proposals to be submitted to the RCAF for a supersonic fighter replacement of the CF-100 (and probably the F-86). The basic requirement was for a two man, twin engine airplane with a supersonic combat radius of 200 nautical miles and a ferry range of 1,500 nautical miles. The crucial requirement, which greatly influenced the aircraft configuration, was maneuverability defined as 2g at M 1.5 at 50,000 ft. without loss of speed or altitude. The program was estimated to involve some 600 aircraft to replace the CF-100 in nine regular and eleven auxiliary squadrons. At a later date the auxiliary squadron requirement was dropped as the airplane was considered too advanced and complicated.

On the basis of the proposals submitted, a design and development contract was awarded in March 1954 which provided for the construction of two prototypes. At the time, it was assumed that the engine would come from the U.K. or U.S. and, likewise, that the fire control system and missile armament would come from the U.S. In May 1954, the design of the airplane designated the CF-105 commenced.

The first major problem to be encountered was the selection of the engine. At first, the best possibility appeared to be the Curtis-Wright J-67, but because of technical difficulties, the timing of its development slipped and this possibility was eliminated. The only other prospect was the Pratt & Whitney J-75. Although it did not meet the exacting requirements of the CF-105, it was chosen to power the two prototypes.

Although the Government decided not to have Orenda develop the engine for the airplane, the company was not prepared to stand idly by and let the design, research and development staff and facilities, built up successfully for over a decade, go down the drain. Accordingly, the company commenced the design of an engine, designated the PS-13, tailored to the requirements of the CF-105. The company entered into this undertaking which was to involve many millions of dollars at its own expense on the basis of its confidence in its own capability.

The second major problem arose out of a report submitted in the fall of 1954 by the National Research Council to the chief of the air staff of the RCAF and to the chairman of the Defence Research Board. The report questioned the performance calculations of the company, particularly the vital drag coefficient, and submitted calculations made by the NRC. There was a considerable discrepancy and, were the figures of NRC to be believed, the company's design was not worthy of being pursued. This presented quite a problem, as the NRC was supposed to be the scientific adviser to the CAS and to the chairman of the DRB.

In addition to the subsonic tests carried out by the NRC, the vital supersonic wind tunnel tests and related work were carried out by the various installations of NACA in the U.S. As a solution to this very delicate problem, the company suggested that the matter be placed before the unquestionable authority of the chairman of NACA in Washington, Dr. Hugh Dryden.

A series of meetings was held in Washington under the auspices and chairmanship of Dr. Dryden attended by all the parties concerned. The outcome was a complete vindication of the company's personnel and their calculations. In fact, NACA considered the figures of the company to be conservative and forecast a more optimistic performance of the aircraft. The company was congratulated for extending the boundaries of the art, particularly in the field of flutter. Dr. Dryden reassured the management of the company of its confidence in its engineers and added that he was unaware of any to be considered their peers. That was the last of many problems with the NRC.

In this period the company attempted to convince the Government to change the approach to the project. Rather than build two prototypes from sketchy engineering and tooling and suffer a lengthy time gap before proceeding with production drawings, it was proposed that engineering and tooling be done on a production basis from the outset. It also followed that a quantity of production airplanes should be ordered. This was the approach being adopted in the U.S. In the light of newly revealed developments with regard to the threat and the desire to accelerate the project, this new approach was adopted by the Canadian Government in March 1955. At first, the quantity was increased from two to five, then to eleven, reduced to eight as a result of an economy wave, then ultimately and finally an additional twenty-nine were added, bringing the total to thirty-seven which total remained until the cancellation. This productionized approach placed even greater onus on the engineers, as their engineering releases and drawings were committed to hard, sophisticated tooling and production. This necessitated extensive component and systems testing before releasing engineering. Much of this testing had been carried out previously in other aircraft projects in an extensive flight testing of prototypes.

Extensive and expensive test facilities were created by the company involving millions of dollars. A building was erected to house the fuel system test rig. Complete aircraft structures could be tested in the huge structural and mechanical test laboratories. Flight simulation was provided by cockpit presentations coupled to complex analogue computation and displays. The entire electrical system was simulated and displayed on test panels. The engineers also had the use of one of the first enormous IBM 704 computers. These test facilities were in addition to those required for production, such as huge skin milling machines, gigantic presses and the most modern machine tool equipment. This new approach also crystalized the engine situation, as Orenda had been test running the PS-13 with outstanding success. It had demonstrated its design performance and, accordingly, became the most powerful engine with the highest performance in the world.

Dry thrust : 19,450 lbs
With afterburner: 25,600 lbs
Weight: 4,800 lbs

Faced with these facts, the Government decided it had little choice but to adopt the engine for the CF-105. In the fall of 1955, the Government contracted for the continued development and preproduction of the engine which was to be installed in the sixth airplane. At the time, the company had some $9,000,000 invested in the design and development of the engine.

The program for the CF-105, christened the Arrow by the RCAF, now involved five airplanes to be powered by J-75 engines, the accelerated development preproduction of the PS-13, named the Iroquois, which was to power the sixth, and all subsequent aircraft, designated Mk-2.

The Fire Control System

The still unresolved question of vital importance was the selection of a fire control system and armament. Lack of this decision affected major elements in the design of the aircraft. The company assumed, however, that only the Hughes MX-1179 electronics system and the Falcon missile was applicable as this was the armament being developed for the USAF and nothing else would be available. Accordingly, the company proceeded with the design on this basis, as best it could, obtaining information from

Hughes through the back door.

It was decided that the missiles would be housed internally in a vast, retractable armament bay in the main undersection of the fuselage, as large as the wartime B-29 bomb bay. Provision was made for either eight Falcon or four Sparrow missiles. Officers of the USAF were particularly interested in this configuration as it would house the atomic bomb of that era.

In due course and to the utter consternation of the company, the RCAF asked Hughes and RCA in the U.S. to submit designs and proposals for a fire control system to meet a specification which they had prepared. The system was to be compatible with the Sparrow II missile being developed by the U.S. Navy. This specification reflected a considerable extension to the state of the art and beyond that which the USAF had dared to venture. Hughes, the chosen instrument of the USAF in this field, endeavored to dissuade the RCAF from their course, to no avail. Hughes submitted its proposal and cost estimate, which was astronomical, and they were rejected. In turn, the RCAF chose the proposal of RCA, as it promised the "pie in the sky" performance desired in the required time and at relatively reasonable cost. It should be mentioned that RCA had virtually no experience in this very specialized field and, consequently, the Canadian Government planned to finance its education, mainly in the U.S.

As officers of the RCAF and engineers of the company had been having a running battle on the subject for months, the chief of the air staff called me to his office to announce his decision and to ask for the cooperation of the company. A last futile attempt was made to change the decision on grounds which seemed obvious and with a concluding warning that this decision would certainly threaten the Arrow program and, hence, the very independence of the RCAF if, indeed, it would not kill both. In spite of all, the CAS was assured of and given the full cooperation of the company. The date of this meeting was July 1956, two years after the start of design of the airplane. The project now involved the design and development of the most advanced supersonic airplane with its advanced powerful engine, as well as the most advanced fire control system conceivable, to be developed in the U.S. with Canadian Government funds.

The U.S. Navy decided to abandon the development of the Sparrow II missile. This occurred in late 1956 at which time the Government decided to take over the development and have it carried out in Canada by Canadair in conjunction with Canadian Westinghouse. The vicious circle was now complete for the development of these four major advanced components.

Decisions with regard to the fire control system and missile were as vital to the future of the Arrow as they were fundamentally wrong. The electronics system, which became known as Astra, was wrong on every count:

1) It was to be undertaken in the U.S. by a company inexperienced in

the field;
2) Timing and costs projected were ridiculous in the opinion of the company with vast experience in the field and on the basis of general experience and common sense;
3) The basic economics were insupportable, regardless of the number of aircraft which could be envisaged;
4) It involved both serious delay and substantial cost increases in the design and development of the airplanes;
5) It was a different system to the one to be used by the USAF fighters operating jointly in NORAD;
6) Although highly desirable, the advanced performance specified could not be justified within the concept of the Arrow project or in the face of reality.

The justification of the requirement was the questionable necessity for the airplane to operate outside the ground radar environment. The USAF however, were also to have some small part in the air defence of North America and, at the that time at least, did not consider that degree of sophistication a necessity.

The technical decision was supported by those officers in the RCAF and the Department of Defence Production who were anxious to put Canada into the age of advanced electronics and missilery. This in itself was a desirable objective but should not have been put on the back of the Arrow project, which was taking Canada into the very exacting realm of supersonic flight. In the U.S. and elsewhere, engines, fire control systems, and air to air missiles are developed for a range of aircraft, thus spreading the costs over a number of aircraft projects.

United Kingdom Interest

In the spring of 1957, the Hon. Reginald Maudling, Minister of Supply in the U.K. visited Malton and was so impressed with the Arrow and the organization that he sent a high level team of some twenty-five experts to assess the possibility of a joint program of production in England. Air Marshal Sir Thomas Pike led the air force team. Sir George Gardiner, head of RAF, led the technical contingent and there was a group of production experts from the Supply Ministry. They spent considerable time at Malton analyzing every aspect of the project: the operational requirement of the RAF, the design and technical side, and a plan for production by stages in England. When they left there was little doubt that the Arrow had passed this scrutiny with flying colours.

Not long after the departure of this team the company was advised to send representatives to the U.K. as a favourable decision appeared imminent. I, accompanied by R.A. Lindley, Avro's chief engineer, followed up this advice. The only outstanding problem for the British was the fire control system. They had no faith in the Astra. It was pointed out, however, that no doubt the Hughes system could be made available. In the midst of the negotiations, an economy wave was announced by the Minister of Defence, deferring a decision on the Arrow. There were some very disappointed air force officers as a result.

Over this period, Avro and Orenda were asked to submit revised cost estimates for design and development and production of various quantities of airplanes, and these costs kept mounting. The total project had grown into very large dimensions and was causing concern in the political circles. It was to be revealed later by the Conservative Minister of National Defence in the hearings of the Special Committee on Defence Expenditure in 1960 that

> The Minister of National Defence, Mr. Campney proceeded to Washington and had discussions with the U.S. Secretary of Air Mr. Quarles. While no record is available of these discussions, it is understood that the U.S. Secretary of Air expressed some concern as to the possibility of the Canadian Government not proceeding with this aircraft (CF-105), as they did not expect anything to appear in the U.S. development field to take the place of the CF-105 to meet the requirements in Canada. However, it is believed that no commitment was received from the U.S. Secretary of Air that the United States would purchase any of these aircraft for their own use.

The Diefenbaker Election and Arrow "Rollout"

The foregoing events in the Arrow project were under the administration of the Liberal Government. June 1957 saw the surprise election of the minority Conservative Government under the leadership of J.G. Diefenbaker. The Minister of National Defence was to be retired army Major-General George Pearkes VC aged seventy. The new Minister of Defence Production to replace C.D. Howe was to be Raymond O'Hurley, ex-timber grader and estimator from Quebec. The Minister of External Affairs was to be Sidney Smith, formerly distinguished president of the University of Toronto.

The first unnecessary debacle of the new Government arose over the actual signature of the NORAD agreement. The previous Liberal Government had agreed in principle but apparently deferred formal signature, pending the oncoming election. The new Liberal leader, Lester Pearson, attacked the new and inexperienced Government on a purely procedural basis. The sad result of their academic political row was the gulf of mistrust it created between the politicians and the military. The chairman of the Joint Chiefs of Staff Committee had apparently advised the incoming Government to sign the agreement for good and practical reasons but was suspected, particularly by the politicians and typically by Diefenbaker, of leading them into a trap. Unfortunately this suspicion and mistrust of not only the military but also the senior civil servants prevailed from the beginning to the end of the Diefenbaker reign.

The first benchmark of the Arrow project was its unveiling to the public on October 4, 1957. The guest of honour and the man who drew the curtain to reveal this masterpiece was the Hon. George Pearkes. In his address he said, in part:

> Much has been said of late about the coming missile age and there have been suggestions from well intentioned people that the era of the manned aeroplane is over and that we should not be wasting our time and energy producing an aircraft of the performance, complexity and cost of the Avro Arrow. They suggest that we should put our faith in missiles and launch straight into the era of push button war. I do not feel that missile and manned aircraft have, as yet, reached the point where they should be considered as competitive. They will in fact become complimentary. Each can do things which the other cannot do and for some years to come both will be required in the inventory of any nation seeking to maintain an adequate deterrent to war.

Air Marshall Campbell, CAS of the RCAF, also addressed the gathering of some 12,000 and said:

> Suffice to say, the planned performance of this aircraft is such that it can effectively meet and deal with any likely bomber threat to this continent over the next decade. We in the Air Force look upon this aircraft as one component of a complex and elaborate air defence system covering, in the first instance, the whole of the North American continent.... Because this aircraft–the Avro Arrow–is a twin engine, two-place machine, and because it will embody what will be the most modern equipment in the airborne interception and fire control fields, it should have an inherent flexibility in operations and promising future development potential. For those reasons we look to it to fill a great need in the air defence system in the years to come.

This does not sound like the man who would reputedly offer advice to the Government within eleven months leading the Government to a decision to cancel the project on strategic grounds.

Other honoured guests attending the ceremony were: Gen. Charles Foulkes, Chairman, Joint Chief of Staff; Dr. Adam Zimmerman, Chairman, Defence Research Board; A/V/M F.R. Miller, Deputy Minister of Defence; A/V/M L.E. Wray, AOC, Air Defence Command; W.H. Huck, Assistant Deputy Minister of Defence Production; General K. Berquist, Deputy Chief of Staff, USAF; General Leon Johnson, USAF. Ironically, it was on this day that the Russians fired their first Sputnik into space.

On January 23, 1958, General Pearkes said in the House of Commons that the future of the Arrow depended "entirely" on the nature of the threat, not on its cost.

First Flight

The second Arrow benchmark was its first flight on March 25, 1958 in the heat of another election campaign.

An Avro employee was to write the following in describing the event:

It is the morning of March 25, 1958, a typical March day, a little raw and slightly overcast. The site is Toronto airport at Malton and, more particularly, the sprawling plant of Avro Aircraft located on the fringe of the airport. On this morning some 9,500 people converge at the plant, as usual, but most of them know this is far from a usual day. The sense of anticipation has existed for several days, but it is felt that this would be "the day".

An eerie feeling runs through the offices. The batteries of typewriters and machines are operating, but the usual rhythmic pace is missing. There is more hushed chatter and intermingling of people than usual.

In the large main engineering department the atmosphere seems to be statically charged. Particularly is this the case in the sections most directly connected with flight. Groups are huddled in solemn conclave poring over drawings and data to ensure in this eleventh hour that all is in order. Every detail is double and triple checked. The tension and anxiety enveloping these men is palpable.

In the shops there is the usual rat-tat-tat of rivet guns, the whirl and hum of machines, and the thunder of gigantic presses, but there is more commotion than normal, more traffic in the aisles and between work stations and more chatter. Expectancy is reflected in the faces of all.

The telemetering labs are located in the vast flight test hangar. Activity here is tense and at a specially high tempo because this department with its intricate equipment represents, in effect, the stethoscope. It monitors every function of the airplane in flight.

The test flight hangar proper is the focal point, the heart beat of this big and anxious organization. Although cluttered with airplanes, there is only one commanding front and center stage, RL201. There she stands, tall, white, and proud. She is being preened. The last company checks have been completed. The company chief inspector has signed her off, "Airworthy, cleared for flight". She is now in the hands of the RCAF for the final check. Then the chief RCAF inspector would countersign the vital document, "Cleared for flight".

The flight test crew hooks the tow bar on to her nose gear and the tractor starts to move her slowly along the taxi strip to the airport. As she passes along the side of the machine shop and assembly bay, people appear from nowhere and every window is full of faces. Although this same procedure had been followed many times previously for engine runs and taxi trials, the log book entry, "Cleared for flight" had been made for the first time and, as if by magic, 9,500 people know it.

The first stop is the engine run-up shed. The flight crew starts the two powerful engines, checks their functions and all systems. All is well. She is ready for flight. Shortly, the incomparable Jan Zurakowski arrives. He checks the airplane thoroughly on the ground. He converses and jokes with the flight crew and the key men in the engineering department. He is satisfied. He is ready. He is happy. He is confident for the greatest flight of his life. He bids farewell and mounts the tall ladder to the cockpit. He settles in and, after a thorough cockpit check, closes the clamshell canopy and locks himself in.

While the magnificent white bird taxies towards the end of the long north-south runway, the company public address system conveys the request to all personnel to proceed in an orderly manner to the tarmac surrounding the end of the assembly bays.

In the meantime, the two chase airplanes, an F-86 and a CF-100, take to the air to observe every minute detail in flight. Six camera crews are positioned to record the event from every angle on the ground.

There she stands, off the end of the runway, with Zura at the controls making a final check for the first flight of Avro Arrow RL201. As she stands with her power plants throbbing, she looks like one beautiful, compact form but the 9,500 people anxiously watching know that that final form was shaped out of some 40,000 parts which they had created and drawn on paper, cut and formed into highly specialized metal, assembled into small and large units, in order to produce that final, complete aerodynamic shape. They knew the miles of wiring strung throughout her body, also, the intricate and precise tubing which had to withstand unbelievable pressures. They knew of the hundreds of pieces of new, exacting equipment created so that she could complete her mission.

The engineers were confident they had done everything within their power to ensure that the airplane would fly according to plan. Although this was the first airplane, it was not a prototype, as such. The drawings were precise production drawings issued only after an exhaustive test program. There had been thousands of hours of wind tunnel testing. Scale models fully instrumented were fired into the air over Lake Ontario propelled by Nike missiles. Every piece of equipment and all systems had been exhaustively proven under simulated conditions of flight. Extreme conditions of temperature, pressure, speed, and altitude had been applied. A complete program of metallurgical testing had been performed to ensure that the metals, some of them new, could sustain extremes of stress and fatigue. Thus, the engineers knew that the airplane had been precisely built since it was made from exact detail production tooling. This was not a hand made prototype. They also knew they had gone beyond the state of the art and ventured into the unknown in some areas. Now, they could only hope and pray.

Some four years of the work of these people was reflected in the airplane standing at the end of the runway. Some $115 million of taxpayers money had been spent. The future of the 9,500 people, the company, the RCAF, and of Canada as a military and high technology industrial power for a decade, was at stake.

Zura turns the Arrow onto the end of the runway facing in the direction of the plant. He accelerates the engines for a final check. The ground shudders and adjacent buildings almost shake as the 40,000 lbs of thrust is battered into the atmosphere. He checks with the telemetering labs, "OK, all clear". He checks with the DOT tower who have cleared the area and handed control to the Avro tower, "All clear for take off". "Roger," replies Zura. With a mighty roar from the engines, the airplane moves down the runway. The movement seems slow and painful at first but then one senses in the pit of ones stomach the acceleration and power. Faster and faster the great white streak thunders down the runway, the knife edge of her delta wings piercing and at the same time clutching the air to lift her thirty ton body into flight. The wheels rise from the ground, a foot at a time. She pauses at ten or twenty feet for some time, accelerating, trying her wings, then, gradually, climbs and flies away.

The cheers and shouts of joy and relief from the crowd fill the vacuum of silence left by the roar of the engines. The emotion and anxiety of these people, building within them for months, explodes and permeates the air around Malton.

The talk between Zura, the CF-100 chase plane, and the tower is ecstatic. The spidery, complex undercarriage retracted and stowed away as planned, just as it had hundreds of times on the test rig. The airplane was flying as predicted, the control surfaces were responding as designed. The flight lasts for thirty-five minutes and is only curtailed when Zura is instructed to land. He circles the airport several times so that those who had created her could see her in her glory. "Prepare to land," from the tower. "Roger" comes the reply and, once again, the crowd grows silent and tense. "Undercarriage down and locked" from Zura and this critical fact is carefully checked and confirmed by the chase plane. He does one last circuit and lines up with the end of the long runway for his approach.

The landing is as crucial as the take off and the Avro people waiting expectantly know it. Their anxiety is reinforced by the readiness of the fire trucks and ambulances with their crews stationed at the side of the runway.

The flaps are down, undercarriage extended and reaching for the ground as the big white, gangling bird glides past the end of the runway. Still at a reasonably high speed she lowers herself slowly, foot by foot onto the cement runway. On touching the ground, small puffs of smoke float out beneath her. In seconds, the red and white braking chute bellows out behind to augment the braking system, bringing the airplane to a safe and smooth stop at, almost, the end of the runway.

Once again, cheers of relief fill the air with the knowledge in the minds of the watchers that she had made it, safe and sound, as they see Zura taxi back to the perimeter of the plant. He pulls her up to the position from which he had taken her. He cuts the engines which continue to whirl and whine as the compressors and turbines continue to spin under their own momentum. He released the canopy, opens it, stands up on his seat and, with a grin from ear to ear, waves to his fellow employees who surround the airplane. The long ladder, again extends to the cockpit, and the triumphant hero starts to descend but not far. The flight crew and engineers clutch and grab at him to hoist him on their shoulders and carry him through the crowd.

The epic first flight completed, the people of Avro know they had a great airplane, the most advanced airplane in the world. They knew there was development yet to be done but they also knew that, basically, they had created a truly great airplane for their country. As they wandered back through the assembly bays, emotionally exhausted, they could see the subsequent aircraft in various stages of completion. Airplane RL202 was in flight test, RL203 was completed and standing at the assembly bay door, RL204 was at the final assembly stage. The employees could see that the whole manufacturing program for thirty-seven airplanes was well in hand.

A first flight is a traumatic event to experience. One must be part of the organization to realize the magnitude of the drama and emotion. This was the first such event for some but not for many others. The latter had taken part in the first flight of the Jetliner on a hot day in August 1949. They had thrilled to the first flight of the CF-100 in January 1950, likewise, to the flight of the first CF-100 Mk-IV in September 1953. The success of this flight and the advanced technology which it demonstrated was the reflection of an accumulation of fifteen years of experience and knowledge.

That flight and the others which quickly followed established the fact that the aircraft met and in many cases exceeded its projected performance. In the initial series of flights, the aircraft flew at 60,000 ft. and at a mach number of 1.75. The aircraft had not been pushed to its maximum capability, even with the Pratt & Whitney engines, which had less power and more weight than the Iroquois. It was obvious that with the Iroquois installed Canada would have the most advanced airplane in the world.

Diefenbaker Re-elected

On March 31, 1958, the Diefenbaker Government was returned with a commanding majority. Its two main problems of defence and the economy could now be faced. When General Pearkes took office, he was generally familiar with the Arrow project but probably unaware that General Norstad, Commander in Chief of the NATO forces, had been pressing for the re-equipping of the RCAF Air Division. Furthermore, Norstad wanted the traditional defensive role of the RCAF changed to an offensive-attack role with nuclear weapons. This request would presumably have been rejected out of hand by the previous Liberal Government since the cornerstone of its policy was that Canada's role would always be defensive. General Pearkes was also to learn that the U.S. had been asking for two Bomarc missile stations to be erected in Canada to plug the gaps in their chain in the U.S.

The period between March and September 1958 saw the completion of three additional Arrows and an acceleration of flying hours, which continued to produce more sensational results, amongst them being flights at Mach 2. Also during this period the companies were asked to provide numerous cost estimates on various numbers of aircraft to be produced. It was obvious that different programs were under active consideration.

The First Tremor

The company had poured millions of dollars into facilities and equipment to engineer, test, and produce the Arrow and Iroquois and was continuing to do so in August 1958, in the midst of the press controversy. There was a degree of protection for the company in these capital expenditures through accelerated depreciation but vast amounts of expenditure were applicable only to these two projects and no protection for capital expenditures was provided in the case of cancellation. I prepared a brief on this subject and submitted it to Mr. O'Hurley in late August. I stated that no further capital expenditure would be made until this problem was resolved. Because of the emphatic manner of Mr. O'Hurley's agreement, I learned for the first time that the Arrow program might be in jeopardy. In reflecting on the matter, it was recalled that the recent attitude of the officers of the RCAF and Defence Production had been cool, if not evasive. As the company could learn nothing from the appropriate ministers, it was felt necessary to seek an audience with the PM. As Mr. Gordon, president of the parent company was in England, Mr. Tory, a director of the parent company, its legal counsel, and a leading Conservative acquainted with Mr. Diefenbaker, undertook this assignment in early September.

In his meeting with the PM, Mr. Tory was indeed informed that the Arrow project was in some jeopardy. The PM arranged for meetings with the Ministers of Finance, Defence, and Defence Production. I accompanied Mr. Tory in these further meetings which took place the same day. The first meeting was with Mr. Fleming. To the remark by me that it would appear that Canada might be about to decide that it could not afford to defend itself, the Minister reacted sharply, while delivering a fierce denial. To the question as to whether or not the Government would be interested in a $350,000,000 reduction in the program's cost of 100 aircraft, Mr. Fleming replied that he would be interested in a reduction of 350 cents. Mr. Fleming was then advised that this $350,000,000 saving could be effected by replacing the Astra system and Sparrow missiles with the Hughes MX-1179 and the Falcon missiles, which ought to have been chosen in the first place. Mr. Fleming demonstrated serious interest in the idea and asked that the suggestion be made to the two ministers we were about to meet.

The meeting with Mr. Pearkes, with Air Marshall Campbell present, was as brief as it was futile. The suggested change of the fire control system and missile was received with utter disdain.

On the contrary, the meeting with Mr. O'Hurley, with his deputy Mr. Golden in attendance, was full of surprises and very productive. Apparently of all the various proposals placed before the Government, none had contained the possibility of a switch in the fire control system and the missile, and the minister asked his deputy why this was so. Mr. Golden remarked that the company was proposing the junking of the electronics and missile systems, which were the technologies of the future, in order to preserve their own products and technologies of the past. He also wondered why the company did not also propose the scrapping of the Iroquois in favour of the J-75. I advised him that the company had already investigated this possibility but had rejected it, as it would involve delay and little saving, if any, but were prepared to explore it again, which it did, with the same results. In the end, the minister asked his deputy to examine the effect of the change of the fire control and missile immediately and to advise what savings could be effected. This was done also by a reluctant RCAF and both confirmed the figures of about $350,0000,000.

Upon his return from the UK, Mr. Gordon submitted a brief to the PM to outline the economics of the Arrow-Iroquois programs. This brief indicated that the projected Arrow-Iroquois five-year program did not exceed the annual costs of the comparable program of the CF-100 and Orenda. The brief also endeavoured to portray the real net costs of the project to Canada by estimating the direct and indirect taxes which would flow back to the Government. For example, the figures were of necessity inflated by a 10% sales tax, which was merely a transfer from one Government department to another.

Mr. Gordon also asked if he could be informed of the current position and intentions of the Government, as he believed he had the right to know since he was responsible for the welfare of thousands of people involved. Apparently the reply to this request was devastating as was the balance of the meeting. It was rumoured in several quarters that if the Arrow had a chance, it was destroyed by this meeting of September 17.

In his memoirs Mr. Diefenbaker commented on the meeting as follows:

> Armed with a detailed brief on why we should continue the Arrow programme, he met me on 17 September. To clear away a misrepresentation of what happened at our meeting, in no sense could it be described as a nasty personal confrontation. I do recall that he began his presentation in a blustering fashion, "Well, I want to tell you" pounding his hand on my desk for emphasis. I stopped him immediately and pointed out that he was liable to do himself serious injury if he kept on banging his hand. That ended his bellicosity.

His brief however was strongly worded. The two companies principally involved would be closed down, there would be mass firings, etc. Projects like the CF-105, however, could hardly be considered as primarily a means of promoting employment. I could agree with Gordon's argument that it was important for Canada to have an independent aircraft industry. If Avro and Orenda went into liquidation, we would still have one: De Havilland would not be affected, nor would the Transport Marine Aircraft Section of Canadair. As to the argument that subsequently became something of a conventional wisdom among critics, that the building of the Arrow had, to use the words of Gordon's brief a serious fundamental relationship with Canada's capacity to realize the vast potential of her endowment within today's framework of rapidly developing technology, this was, and is nonsense. Modern technology is important to the Canadian economy so far as it can contribute to the growth of Canadian industry and the gross national product. A.V. Roe, since the end of the Second World War had lived and grown rich on Canadian defence contracts. The company seemed horror-struck at the prospect of having ever to compete in a normal market-place situation. As one of the Avro officials explained to General Pearkes in February 1959, his company was not accustomed to doing business in a 'normal commercial way'. They apparently had no intention of even trying to do so.

It is difficult to understand his remark that, "The company seemed horror-struck at the prospect of having ever to compete in a normal market place situation". The company to which he referred, A.V. Roe Canada Ltd. was one of the largest, certainly the most diversified, industrial organizations in Canada, dealing in diverse commercial markets, as has been previously illustrated.

Avro and Orenda were the industrial arm of the RCAF and servants of the Government, as is any purely defence contractor. The companies had fulfilled this role solely from their inception and for a period of fifteen years.

As Parliament was in recess, the PM called a press conference on September 23, 1958 to make a statement on defence policy. In essence, the statement said and/or implied the following:

1. The Government had reviewed the Air Defence Program. "In doing so, it had detailed advice from its military experts on the nature of attacks on North America . . . ."
2. "That the number of supersonic interceptor aircraft required for the RCAF air defence command will be substantially less than could have been foreseen a few years ago, if in fact such an aircraft will be required at all in the 1960s . . . ."
3. "The preponderance of expert opinion is that by the 1960s manned aircraft, however outstanding, will be less effective in meeting the threat than previously expected."
4. Regarding the Bomarc missile, "This is a long range, anti-aircraft

missile . . . . It can be used with either a conventional high explosive warhead or a nuclear warhead."
5. "In order that the Pinetree radar system may be able to deal more effectively with the increased speed and numbers of aircraft to be controlled and with the introduction of the Bomarc guided missile, the Government has decided to install the 'SAGE' electronic control and computing equipment in the Canadian air defence system."
6. "The nine Canadian air defence squadrons already equipped with CF-100 aircraft will continue in their present role pending their replacement with Bomarc weapons or squadrons with later types of aircraft . . . ."
7. "In view of the introduction of missiles into the Canadian air defence system and the reduction in the expected need for a manned, supersonic, interceptor aircraft, the Government has decided that it would not be advisable at this time to put the CF-105 into production. The Government believed, however, that to discontinue abruptly the development of this aircraft and its engine, with its consequent effects upon the industry, would not be prudent with the international outlook as uncertain and tense as it is. As a measure of insurance with present tensions as they are, therefore, the Government has decided that the development program for the Arrow aircraft and Iroquois engine should be continued until next March, when the situation will be reviewed again in the light of all the existing circumstances at that time."
8. "Although both the Arrow aircraft and Iroquois engine appear now to be likely to be better than any alternative expected to be ready by 1961, it is questionable whether in any event their margin of superiority is worth the very high cost of producing them by reason of the relatively small numbers likely to be required."
9. He then announced the cancellation of the Astra system and the Sparrow missile at a saving of about $330,000,000 in a program of one hundred aircraft. He said the airplane would be modified to accommodate a system and missile in production in the U.S. (Hughes MX-1179 and Falcon).
10. The PM said that about $303 million had been spent on the Arrow program to date and, with the Astra and Sparrow, the cost per plane for one hundred operational aircraft would be about $12,500,000 but, by substituting the alternative fire control and missile, the cost per plane would be about $9,000,000. He did not elaborate on the make-up of the figures.
11. For future reference another statement should be added, "while Canada's role in the coming age of missiles is entirely a defensive

one . . . ."
12. "It now seems evident that in the larger weapons systems now required for air forces, Canadian work in design, development, and production of defence equipment will have to be closely integrated with the major programs of the U.S. The U.S. Government recognizes this and they are now prepared to work out production sharing arrangements with us."

This was not, nor was it designed to be, a clear statement of Government defence policy. It was obviously a contrived and deliberately misleading political pronouncement concerning defence, to fulfil purely political objectives. The statement contained errors and evident contradictions, which in detail were the following:

- The statement was designed to give the impression that it reflected the views of the military, which was not the case. It over inflated the importance of the missile, inaccurately, for the purpose of down grading, or even eliminating the manned aircraft.
- It said that much fewer aircraft would be required, if any, and if in fact this was true what was the purpose of signing the NORAD agreement in May 1958, just four months earlier. NORAD was established primarily to integrate and control the operational defensive air forces of the U.S. and Canada meaning, basically, men flying airplanes.
- Although there were to be fewer aircraft, if any, the reason for providing extension of the Pinetree radar system was "to deal more effectively with the increased speed and numbers of aircraft."
- The Bomarc was referred to as a "long range anti-aircraft missile". Not true, as the Bomarc was considered, in the broader sense, as a relatively short range missile, with a range of some 200-400 miles.
- It was implied that the Bomarc was interchangeable, as between a conventional and nuclear warhead. Not true. The Bomarc A missile had a conventional warhead, while the Bomarc B, which was the one chosen, had a nuclear warhead only.
- If, in fact, there was no practical need for an interceptor anti-bomber weapon due to the introduction of intercontinental ballistic missiles, then why adopt an unproven new and complex anti-bomber missile, with limited range, from fixed positions, and only effective with a nuclear warhead?
- The justification for continuing the Arrow and Iroquois seemed to be shaky in the light of all the previous remarks. Any change in the tense international situation six months hence, in March 1959, could have little bearing in the matter, as the airplanes were not to be

operational until 1961. Between September 19, 1958 and February 19, 1959 the PM must have changed his mind in regard to abrupt discontinuation and the effect on the industry.

- In dealing with costs, the PM referred to a quantity of one hundred aircraft. What had happened to the requirement to replace the nine CF-100 and six F-86 squadrons in NORAD and the four CF-100 and eight F-86 squadrons in NATO, a compliment of some one thousand airplanes? What consideration was given to the possible requirements of others?
- At the time of this statement the RCAF was still to take the final delivery of the subsonic CF-100 and F-86, yet it was implied that the Mach 2 Arrow would probably not be required, less than three years hence, on strategic grounds.
- The staggering unit cost of $9,000,000 results from piling on to the relatively small quantity of one hundred aircraft the cost of design development, tooling, spares, ground handling equipment, etc. Even so, the costs seemed unduly inflated. He implied that Canada could not undertake major weapons systems development in the future and that industry would have to act as sub-contractors to the U.S. industry, under the banner of "production sharing". This might have been true of the future but had no bearing on the Arrow-Iroquois projects, as their technical ability had been demonstrated, the designs were virtually completed, and development was well in hand. $300,000,000 had already been spent in this connection. The company took a more optimistic view, possibly borne out of wishful thinking. The development of the airplane and the engine and the production of thirty-seven aircraft was continuing. The company was hopeful that costs could be reduced and, regardless of the double-talk, it knew that the primary weapon for the air defence of North America was and would continue to be the manned interceptor. It knew that every responsible officer in the RCAF, the USAF and NORAD were of this opinion. The Hughes fire control system and missile were to be installed. The company immediately took steps, however, again to determine the true position and Government intentions.

Reprieve

I went to Ottawa to meet Blair Fraser of the *Financial Post* and Michael Barkway of the *Financial Times*, deans of the Ottawa press corps and specialists in matters of defence. They were positive in their opinion that, for all practical purposes, the Arrow project was finished and was being kept alive over the winter months in consideration of the unemployment situation. When asked why they were so certain, they said it was reflected in the attitude of the PM during the press conference. Furthermore, this advice had been leaked by one or more of the Ministers. Apparently, the Ministers would talk more freely with the press than they would with the company.

The next meeting was with Howard Green, Minister of Public Works and acting PM. Mr. Diefenbaker was away on a European tour. He said, in effect, that he was unable to add anything to the PM's statement, which spoke for itself. Other meetings were held with Messrs Pearkes, O'Hurley and Hees, when the same general theme was taken; however, they all vehemently denied that the Arrow was in effect cancelled. The impression gained from this series of meetings and others which followed was that the RCAF had not stated a requirement for the Arrow and if a requirement by the Military was established and if costs could be reduced, there was every likelihood that the airplane would be produced.

The next series of meetings was with the Military: General Foulkes, chairman of the Joint Chiefs of Staff Committee, Air Marshal Campbell, and Adam Zimmerman, chairman of the DRP. When asked for his interpretation of the PM's statement, the General replied, "a masterpiece of subterfuge". Apart from this remark, their views and opinions were guarded, but one point was unanimously clear–the primary weapon for the air defence of Canada was the manned interceptor. They said the problem was not military, but one of economics and politics.

Upon return to my office in Malton, I was greeted with the resignations of the VP of engineering of Orenda and others. They would not accept the company's interpretation of the situation. They had had enough. They would not continue to pour their hearts and souls into a project which had become a game of political charades. I asked them if they were told the position directly by a Minister of the Crown, would they reconsider? They agreed and they were told by Mr. O'Hurley that the Arrow in effect was not cancelled, that if there was a military requirement and if the costs could be reduced, the project would proceed. They accepted that statement in good faith.

As may be imagined, the development of a large complex supersonic airplane and its engine is a very difficult and trying undertaking under the best of conditions, so the added strain may be understood when the daily press are saying that one's efforts and achievements are worthless and should be done away with.

The next mission took me and my assistant, a former Assistant Secretary of the USAF for Research and Development, to Washington to endeavour to ascertain the outcome of Mr. Pearke's visit there in August. Meetings took place with an Assistant Secretary of the USAF. In an effort to reduce costs and to have some U.S. participation, I asked if the USAF would supply, free, the fire control system and missiles and if they would allow the free use of their flight test center at Muroc Lake in California. They said they would be happy to grant this request. They said it would be improper for them to volunteer this offer to the Canadian Government but the company was free to advise the Government that any request of this nature would be looked upon favourably by the Secretary of the USAF.

A letter in regard to the USAF offer was immediately delivered to Mr. O'Hurley by me. Its existence was denied later by Mr. Pearkes in a hearing of the Committee of Defence Expenditures in July 1960, as follows

> The United States, at no time, would consider the purchase or make any contribution towards the development of this aircraft. They were quite prepared to sell us any parts that we needed--and, of course, some parts had to be obtained from the United States--but there was no indication at any time that they made a financial or other contribution

5

CANCELLATION

September 1958—February 1959

This period, between September 23, 1958 and February 20, 1959, the date of the cancellation, witnessed growing and heated debate over the Arrow and all of its aspects. The press featured and inflamed the debate, one of the highlights being a front page editorial, complete with photos, by the publisher of the *Toronto Telegram*, Mr. Bassett. Headlined, "Here are the facts on the Arrow", the photos were of the Arrow and the U.S. built F-106. The theme of the article was that the Arrow was too expensive and that the Government should buy the F-106 from the U.S. There was no question as to the need of an interceptor.

News stories quoted statements made by responsible military authorities to the effect that the need for a manned interceptor was unquestionable and would remain so for the foreseeable future. General Partridge, Commander in Chief of NORAD and his Deputy, Air Marshal Slemon, the unquestionable authorities in the air defence of North America, were outspoken in their opinion to this effect. The Canadian military authorities of course were gagged, but the Defence Minister, Mr. Pearkes, told the House of Commons on November 25, "that manned interceptors would continue to be needed in the foreseeable future." All of these statements were at cross purposes with that of the PM on September 23. Some cracks in the rationale of that statement were beginning to appear in public.

In the light of these circumstances, Avro and Orenda undertook detailed reviews of the costs, on the assumption that the number of aircraft involved was one hundred, in addition to the thirty-seven on order. The unions were appraised of the situation and reacted magnificently in the joint effort to cut and hold costs. In order to eliminate any uncertainty, it was decided voluntarily to submit a fixed price for the complete operational airplane, including the fire control system. This involved the Company in unprecedented risk, but it was considered that it was better to run the risk of breaking the company in this fashion than to stand by and see it die by other means. The price submitted to the Minister was $3,500,000. This eliminated any further speculation of the cost of one hundred airplanes complete. This price would have been $500,000 less had the U.S. supplied the fire control system.

At about the same time, November 19, 1958, the company submitted revised performance figures to the RCAF, which were as follows:

Arrow 2
Combat radius of action at 67,500 lbs max take off weight.
1. Subsonic high altitude mission
    subsonic combat: 589 nautical miles
    supersonic combat (1.5 mach): 506 n.m.
2. Supersonic (1.5 m) high altitude mission
    supersonic combat (1.5m): 358 n.m.
    supersonic combat: 338 n.m.
3. Combat air patrol
    supersonic combat (1.5m) 620 n.m.
4. Subsonic low level (10,000 ft)
    supersonic combat (1.5m): 396 n.m.
5. Ferry mission Range: 1,500 n.m.

Arrow 2A
1. Supersonic (1.5m) high altitude mission
    supersonic combat (1.5m): 500 n.m.
2. Long range mission - subsonic (.92m)
    supersonic combat (1.5m): 685 n.m.

In the CBC television series "The Tenth Decade" Mr. Diefenbaker stated, "It [the Arrow] could not fly further than 150 or 200 miles at fighting speed". He reiterated this range data in his memoirs, "The CF-105 would be able to do nothing but intercept, and that within a very sophisticated ground environment and only within a range of 150 to 200 miles from its base".

Plans for the development of the Arrow were under discussion with the RCAF even prior to the first flight of the Mk1 in early 1958. The lead time on military projects makes it essential to plan far ahead for possible developments to update performance as defence requirements change. With this in mind the company had tabled with the RCAF the following suggested improvements to later Marks of the Arrow.

Arrow 2A: This version incorporated relatively minor changes to the Mk 2 including the provision of extra fuel tankage for increased range, increase in gross weight, resulting in some modifications to the landing gear, and the fitting of variable geometry jet pipe nozzles. Any or all of these modifications would have been retrofitted to the Mk 2 Arrow, giving improved performance.

Arrow Mk 3: This development would have increased the speed of the aircraft from 2M to 3M and the combat altitude from 60,000 ft to 70,000 ft. The modifications in this version were a little more extensive and included uprated Iroquois 3 engines with additional thrust, additional structural insulation to deal with the higher speed, variable geometry engine intakes, plus the modifications listed above for the Mk 2A. The basic geometry of the aircraft would have been unchanged from the Mk 2 and retrofit at some stage in the life of the Mk 2 would have been possible and practical if this was required. The Mk 3 version would have been available by mid 1961 if the threat had increased by that time to require such an aircraft. It is now interesting to compare the characteristics of these versions of the Arrow, which could have been available by 1961, with the three relatively new aircraft being considered by the Canadian Government for operation almost twenty years later.

The company submitted a brochure to the Government outlining various alternative programs which could supplement the Arrow project and which could provide continuity of employment, even if no additional Arrows were ordered beyond the thirty-seven. The company repeatedly pointed out that no alternative program could be devised to preserve the organization should the contract be cancelled outright.

We, in the normal course, had many contacts and meetings with the appropriate Ministers and senior Government officials, but, under these conditions, the conversations were a one-way street. The company tried to be helpful by making suggestions. It was of course trying to promote the case for the Arrow or, failing that, a manned interceptor. The company personnel were obviously anxious and endeavoured to ascertain the true position, so that appropriate steps could be taken in preparation. On more than one occasion I pleaded with the Minister of Defence to tell me if the contracts were, in effect, cancelled or were about to be cancelled so that the company could work with the Government in the orderly wind down or termination of the work. These pleas always fell on deaf ears.

From the day of the election of the Diefenbaker Government, there was virtually no interchange, as between the Government and the company. The company was cut off, more so than the military, for the same reason-- suspicion. The company like the military was a product of the Liberal Government. For their efforts, the company executives were chastised and branded as lobbyists. The company had every right to be involved and should have been consulted, as it had been in the past. The companies were the designers and producers of the airplane and its engine and did feel responsible for the welfare of its 15,000 people. A large body of the personnel had a deep interest and concern for the defence of the country. This concern and commitment was one of the reasons they were devoting their talents to the creation and production of advanced military equipment.

In the past, it was the Government's practice to appropriate funds for each fiscal year ending March 31. These amounts were established as ceilings in the contracts from year to year. Traditionally these limits were exceeded, usually due to the Government's cumbersome paper system, but this was understood and agreed to by the appropriate Government officials. Technically, in the strictest, legal sense the Government was not bound to reimburse the company above the limits in the contract.

In January, 1959 it became apparent that some of the contract limits were about to be exceeded. The amount was estimated to be approximately $20,000,000 by the end of March. There would be an additional amount of some $40,000,000 in outstanding commitments. As indicated previously, in the past the company would carry the over run with the concurrence of the Government.

The situation was now very different. The officers of the Department of Defence Production would not or could not discuss the matter as all matters concerning the Arrow were in the hands of the politicians. I was unable to contact the acting Minister of that Department, Mr. Green, as he refused to see me. In desperation I wrote a letter dated February 9, 1959 to the Minister outlining the situation and saying that, although technically the contracts do not authorize it, the company is carrying on the work on the assumption the Government wished it to do so. Of course, no reply was received but the letter was subsequently tabled in the House, as a feeble attempt to justify the Government's claim that the company knew that the contract was to be cancelled.

Another episode which apparently enraged the PM was his suspicion that the company was to embark on a TV campaign in support of the Arrow. The facts in the case were different. A year or so earlier and before the start of the controversy the company had produced a documentary film, "The Jet Age", for release to interested parties. Prior to September 23, 1958, this film was brought up to date as a contribution commemorating the Fiftieth Year of Flight.

Solely due to the sensitive atmosphere, however, the company thought that before releasing the film it should be cleared with the Government. Accordingly I took the matter up with Mr. Pearkes who was not interested in discussing it, did not wish to see it, and said that it was the complete responsibility of the company. It was not released.

As mentioned previously, it became impossible for the company to deal with the Government. There was the problem of the financial limitations.

The Government had not obtained clearance for the company to deal with Hughes concerning the fire control system and missile. The Government was to decide within thirty days the destiny of the company and the employees. Once again it was decided that the only course open to the company was an approach to the PM. Mr. Tory was again granted that privilege, provided he would come alone. He was not to be accompanied by an officer of the company.

Mr. Tory's report of the meeting with the PM was to the effect that it appeared unlikely that the airplane would be put into production, nevertheless, he was optimistic that thirty-seven airplanes and their engines would be completed, in order to afford the companies the opportunity of undertaking alternative projects. As Mr. Tory was recognized as one of the best legal minds in the country, there could be little doubt as to the accuracy of his impressions. This meeting took place in the first week of February, 1959.

Prior to this meeting, the company had been confident that the Arrow would be produced and had given this assurance to its employees. It still believed that right was might. No lack of optimism, had it existed, could have been conveyed to the employees, as the companies would have fallen apart. This was not a normal manufacturing operation, the engineers and test pilots were constantly under tremendous pressure and strain in probing into the unknown in this demanding, exacting science, and they were dedicated to this national purpose. Also involved was the daily risk of lives.

The confidence of the company was based on the following facts
1. The primary basic military requirement, as stated by the RCAF, was for a manned interceptor, preferably, the Arrow.
2. The costs and economics had been reduced to an acceptable scale and did not exceed the annual costs of a previous comparable program.
3. Two Bomarc stations and the subsonic CF-100 were utterly inadequate for the future defence of the country and no responsible Government would deliberately expose the country to this risk.
4. The Government would not renege on Canada's responsibility in the joint defence of North America.
5. It would not abandon the design and development policy, and the highly skilled technical staffs created to sustain it, thus divesting the country of this last vestige of independence in its defence.
6. Five aircraft were flying and demonstrating, beyond any doubt the outstanding performance and capability of the Arrow. The sixth airplane, with the Iroquois engine, was at the door of the final assembly bay and the balance of the thirty-seven airplanes were in advanced stages of completion.
7. Because of the approach taken to the project, a great deal of the design, test, and development had been accomplished and something in the

order of $400,000,000 had been spent.

February 20, 1959

In his statement of September 23, 1958, the PM had said that the air defence situation would be reviewed in March 1959. Apparently, because of the wide speculation in the press, most of which called into question the validity of his strategic pronouncements in September, arbitrarily, he decided to cancel the contracts. As will be seen later, the review never did take place.

At 10:00 am on Friday, February 20, 1959, the Assistant Deputy Minister of the Department of Defence Production, Gordon Hunter, telephoned me to advise me of the following:

> The PM is making a statement in Parliament on the Arrow project and in essence it is that the Arrow and Iroquois are cancelled as of now and the usual telegrams of termination are being dispatched. ALL WORK IS TO BE STOPPED FORTHWITH AND NO FURTHER COSTS ARE TO BE INCURRED. NO OTHER WORK WILL BE MADE AVAILABLE TO THE COMPANIES.

The statement is a declaration, in my opinion, of Canada's intent to join the Third World.

I immediately met with Mr. Gordon and other senior officers of the company. Details of the PM's statement were received from the Canadian press. The telegrams were not received until about 1:00 pm and were the standard form of termination instructions.

The first problem, of course, was what to do with 15,000 employees with only relatively meagre work to do. The telegrams were most specific, "all work on the Arrow and Iroquois was to stop forthwith and no further costs were to be incurred." No other work was to be made available, and it was clear that the advanced technology work being carried out by the companies on behalf of the Government was at an end. The work remaining might occupy 2,000 to 3,000 people, but which ones? The seniority provisions in the union contracts went back to the days of Victory Aircraft at the end of the war. After much deliberation, the conclusion was reached reluctantly that no alternative was available, other than give notice to all employees, with the exception of the supervision and some senior engineers.

I relayed this conclusion to Mr. Hunter at about 2:00 pm. It was emphasized to him that this was not to be construed as putting pressure on the Government, and no other motive was involved. It was, simply, that no other course was open in the light of the Government's instructions. He was asked to inform the PM in case this action was not in accord with his wishes. I said that, unless instructions to the contrary were received by 4:00

pm, notice would be given over the company's public address systems at 4:00 pm. The announcement said that the seniority records were being reviewed and those for whom work was available, would be notified as soon as possible. Some 2,500 were recalled.

As one may imagine, this event caused an uproar. Protests and demands came from every corner. Malton must be preserved, particularly, the technical organizations, but it was too late. The headlines in the Toronto press that night and the following day were black with ink in three inch type. The Ontario Legislature was called in special session early the following week to listen to the demands of the Opposition and to hear the soothing words of the Premier, Leslie Frost, who gave the assurance that Canadians, being sound and reasonable people, Malton would be reconstituted and the great technical organizations would be preserved. He undertook to assure this through the representations he would make to the federal Government.

Saturday, February 21, Mr. Gordon was in contact with the PM who said he would send the Ministers of Finance and Labour, Messrs Fleming and Starr, to confer with the company the next day. This was the first time since June 1957 that the Government condescended to confer with the company. This meeting was to be held in Mr. Tory's office in Toronto. As the CBC documentary commemorating the fiftieth anniversary of the first flight in Canada was scheduled to be shown at the time of the meeting, a TV set was installed in the office. It was ironic to be watching the development of aviation in Canada over fifty years, particularly the part pertaining to Avro, the formal burial of which was being arranged by the participants in the meeting. Arrangements were made also for Mr. Gordon and me to meet with the PM on February 24.

In the midst of this turmoil, the company received phone calls from the U.S. Space Agency, NASA, as well as from U.S. aircraft manufacturers to extend sympathy but also to ascertain if the brains would be available for export. The company said they were and would do what it could to place its key people in U.S. projects where they would be appreciated. The exodus started on Monday, February 23.

In the Commons on Monday, February 23, the PM released a tirade against the company. He said that the company's action "was cavalier, so unreasonable, that the only conclusion any fair-minded person can come to is that it was done for the purpose of embarrassing the Government." He went on to say, "We will also give consideration to any suggestions that may be made to alleviate the particularly disastrous conditions under which various employees find themselves as a result, not of our action--for that action we gave notice last September–but the precipitate, unwarranted and unjustifiable action on Friday last of discharging these employees who had been faithful over the years, without regard to any considerations".

In a further feeble attempt to shift responsibility on to the company he said,

> The statement has been made that there have been no discussions and that there was no prior knowledge. I ask the vice president of the company whether or not on two or more occasions he had not fully discussed it with members of the Government and whether there was any doubt in his mind as to whether or not a decision was to be made. Indeed, during the past few months Mr. Smye, one of the vice presidents of Avro, spoke to the Minister of Transport (Mr. Hees) about the possibility of the Government giving encouragement to the production of civil aircraft at the Avro plant.

The results of discussions with members of the Government have already been revealed. Certainly the company knew a decision was to be made. That was not the point at issue. The question was, what decision? Mr. Diefenbaker tried to imply that the company knew the decision was to cancel the Arrow which was not true.

Discussions had been held with Mr. Hees to ascertain the Government's attitude concerning the development of a jet aircraft to replace the Viscount, in time, meaning two to three years hence. This was to be a project to follow the Arrow after completion of the thirty-seven, one hundred and thirty-seven, or more. Neither this project, nor any other, would fill the vacuum resulting from an immediate termination.

The gist of the PM's statement in the House was that the Arrow project, in effect, had been cancelled in September 1958, and that the company had been given notice to this effect in his statement of September 23. Further, that the company knew it was to be cancelled but still had not come forward with any alternative projects to provide continuing employment. In other words, the full responsibility for the disastrous conditions at Malton was that of the company.

In reply to the PM's statement, a Liberal member, George McIlraith, said,

> The Minister of National Defence, as recently as November 25 said—and I am referring to the press conference statement—that the RCAF would require a manned interceptor for some years to come. This statement was made right after similar comment by Air Marshal Slemon. I quote the Minister of National Defence: 'what we decided last September was not to produce the Arrow under conditions which surrounded Arrow production at that time, but to re-examine the cost and then we would know where we are going'. That was his statement and I have no criticism of him for having made the statement at that time in that way. However, I do have a criticism for the PM now tonight, seeking to indicate that the company should have known since last September that this contract was to be cancelled.

The entire responsibility for the "cavalier and so unreasonable precipitate, unwarranted and unjustifiable action" was that of the Government. In fact, there are no words to describe adequately the enormity of this disastrous act.

The Government decreed that no work was to be performed. With no work to be performed, the company had no alternative but to give notice and to reimburse the employees accordingly under the terms of the union agreements. Mr. Diefenbaker said, "All of the employees will be entitled to approximately three weeks salary or wages. Why rush them out on Friday afternoon?" This remark regarding termination pay is incorrect and irrelevant to the matter of giving notice to the employees. Mr. Diefenbaker's implied generosity did not stand the test of reality as it was only after a court case that the Government paid the termination allowances recommended by the company for monthly paid staff.

At 10:00 am on Tuesday, February 24, Mr. Gordon and I met with the PM and Messrs Pearkes, O'Hurley, Fleming Hees, and Starr. It was a pretty sad performance. Mr. Gordon and I were chastised by the PM. In concluding his dissertation, he waved his finger in a menacing fashion and declared that the company knew the contract was going to be cancelled. He was then asked who in the company knew it was going to be cancelled as neither Mr. Gordon nor I did, and he replied that Mr. Tory knew. As the PM advised the press, this had been an exploratory meeting and the company representatives would now meet with various Ministers.

The problem with the other meetings was the complete ignorance of the Ministers as to the function and methods of industry. They thought projects and work could be turned on and off like a tap. It was explained to them that nothing could be done immediately to solve the problem. Further, it was suggested that there was a requirement for a strike fighter but that work could only commence on that in due course. This suggestion was rejected as being premature. It was proposed that design of a commercial jet for TCA to replace the Viscount might be undertaken. This was encouraged and the company was asked to take it up with the president of the airline, Gordon McGregor. This was subsequently done, with the anticipated results. Mr. McGregor informed me that a team of British Aircraft Corporation engineers had just left with the outline of a design for TCA, together with a letter of intent, which the British company waved at the U.K. Government, who promptly awarded them a design and development contract for the airplane.

The outcome of three or four days of meetings with the Ministers and a further meeting with the PM was that a nucleus of engineers would be retained in both companies for a period of six months, the costs of which was to be shared by the Government and the company. The Government went along with this idea in response to the pressure of the two Conservative Toronto papers and the Ontario Government. The company had no idea what the engineers were to do but in any event it would provide a breathing space. Other matters were discussed, such as procedure and mechanics of carrying out the termination.

We were asked to draft a joint statement on the outcome of the deliberations, which proved to be a difficult assignment. For example, the Government would not agree to say that the retention of the engineering staff and facilities was in the national interest, on the grounds that everything which the Government does is in the national interest. The final draft was left with Mr. Fleming just before our departure by train for Toronto. He was to check with the company by phone in the morning, before it was to be made by the PM in Parliament.

On returning to Malton, the company officers were greeted by the Defence Production Department representative who extended his sympathy for the failure of the mission. He was referring to the fact that during the meeting with the Minister, the Treasury Board, on which some of them sat, had again refused to raise the financial limitations, to which previous reference has been made. This meant that the Government would restrict its responsibility to those amounts. This action was in direct conflict with the basis and spirit of the conversations in Ottawa as well as with the PM's statement to the effect that all costs, properly incurred, would be paid and that funds had been provided for this purpose.

When Mr. Fleming called me to read the almost unrecognizable statement, I made reference to the action of the Treasury Board. His response was that it had not been discussed while in Ottawa which was, technically, true. He said he must leave to go to the House as he, in the absence of the PM, was to make the statement. He added that he would have Mr. O'Hurley call, which he did immediately. Mr. Gordon took over the conversation and told Mr. O'Hurley to ensure that a telegram authorizing the raising of the limits, over his signature or that of his deputy, was received by 4:00 pm, or he would call a press conference and expose the true facts in the Arrow saga. Mr. O'Hurley begged ignorance of the whole matter and said he would have his deputy, Mr. Golden, call which he did, immediately. The situation was explained to Mr. Golden who thought that the demand was unreasonable and almost impossible of fulfillment. Mr. O'Hurley phoned me, however, at 4:00 pm to assure me that all reasonable costs would be paid and that a telegram to this effect was being despatched. This was no small matter, involving as it did the very integrity of the Government and the survival of the company.

In Volume 3 of *One Canada* Mr. Diefenbaker accused the company of "political blackmail" in connection with the cancellation of the CF-100 Mk 6. This accusation was without foundation. The incident referred to above in connection with the cancellation of the Arrow is the only moment in the history of the company when it stooped to political blackmail, which proved to be the only language the politicians understood.

Post-Cancellation Consequences

In carrying out the termination activities, the question arose as to the disposition of the five flying airplanes and ten completed engines. After some delay the Government issued instructions to scrap them. This was refused. I was then told that, if this action was not taken, the Army would be sent in to act. With that threat I capitulated. This was a terrible mistake, one which I will regret for the rest of my life. The instructions were not restricted to the airplanes and engines and their components but to everything--drawings, technical data, micro-film, photos, models, etc. The existence of the airplane and the engine was to be erased without trace. $400,000,000 of the taxpayer's investment in advanced technology was deliberately destroyed. Not the slightest attempt was made to salvage anything from this gigantic investment.

It is impossible to convey the scenes which prevailed in these two enormous, empty plants: Avro, 1,600,000 sq ft, and Orenda 1,200,000 sq ft; a relative handful of dejected employees, scattered here and there, endeavouring to do their little bit of work; the big skin milling machines standing idle, with partially processed aluminum slabs lying on their beds; the gigantic presses standing hauntingly still. At the assembly bay door stood the first Iroquois-powered Arrow and, behind it, stood more in various stages of completion. The silence was deafening. Row upon row of the most modern machine tools stood idle in both plants with their work partly finished. In the flight test hangar stood the five majestic Arrows which had flown above 50,000 ft at twice the speed of sound. They were awaiting the arrival of the blow torches in the hands of the men who built them.

At about this time Sir Roy Dobson arrived from the U.K. to survey the wreckage. He had conversations with the Government leading him to the opinion that the management was not without blame. Mr. Gordon and particularly myself wished Dobson to state the true facts in the case so that the company might retain some respect in the eyes of its shareholders and employees. Well aware of the facts he, nevertheless, refused to air them publicly as it would call into question the integrity of the Government. Other divisions of the parent company, rail cars, buses, steel rails, ship construction and repairs, coal, etc. also had dealings with the Government, and he believed he could live with the Government. In line with this policy, he asked for Mr. Gordon's resignation.

The A.V. Roe exodus had already been well underway since Monday, February 23. Jim Chamberlain, the Chief Technician, who had been with the company from the start and in charge of aerodynamics for the Jetliner, CF-100, and Arrow, went to NASA in a senior capacity. Mr. Chamberlain's contribution to the U.S. space program can best be illustrated by quoting a most unusual document presented to him. It reads:

> National Aeronautics and Space Administration Manned Spacecraft Centre presents this certificate of commendation to James A. Chamberlain for his outstanding contribution to this nation's space flight programs, for the technical direction and leadership of the Project Mercury, for his creation and promotion of the Gemini concept and for his guidance in the design of all manned spacecraft used in the United States' exploration of space to date.
>
> Signed Robert R. Gilruth,
> Director, Manned Space Center.

In the motorcade along Pennsylvania Avenue in Washington, to celebrate the historic space flight by John Glenn, Mr. Chamberlain rode in the second car.

About thirty of the key people at Avro went along with Mr. Chamberlain to take important posts in NASA's space program. R.A. Lindley, Chief Engineer, went to McDonnell Aircraft to work on Project Gemini. He in the industry and Jim Chamberlain at NASA made quite a team. In a discussion with Mr. Lindley, he remarked to me that it was difficult to concentrate on his space project because of the constant questions from engineers working on the F-4. He added that he had not previously realised the Arrow was so advanced.

The U.S. F-105?

In contemplating the immediate problems and the future under relatively calmer conditions, an idea emerged that would have provided a partial solution. It was understood that the Government was to change the role of the RCAF in Europe and that a so-called "strike fighter" would be required. The airplane chosen by the USAF for its role in this theatre was the Republic F-105. Since this airplane was in production in Republic's plant on Long Island, New York, a production sharing scheme might be worked out. Furthermore, it might be possible to install the Iroquois engine. This suggestion was conveyed to Mundy Peale, president of Republic, who was most receptive. The executives and senior engineers of Avro and Orenda set off for Long Island for a series of meetings with Mr. Peale and his team, who proved to be enthusiastic over the possibility of installing the more powerful Iroquois and agreed to a plan of sharing and coordinating production of the airplane. They were prepared to transfer tooling and material immediately to Avro, who would produce components for the current USAF contract. This would have provided work and employment at Avro in a matter of days. Orenda could carry on and complete the development of the Iroquois and put it into production.

As Mr. Frost, the Ontario Premier, had undertaken to do what he could to reconstitute Malton, it was thought he would be interested in endorsing this scheme. A meeting was arranged with Mr. Frost, attended by John Bassett in the capacity of his aviation adviser and myself. The merits of the proposal were realised and appreciated: the air forces, operating in generally the same area, would be operating common equipment; Orenda could be completely reconstituted; Avro could immediately have production work. It seemed a perfect solution and the opinion was expressed by me that, that was its only defect.

On Mr. Frost's behalf, Mr. Bassett proceeded to Ottawa to place the proposal before the PM and the Minister of Defence. Subsequently, Mr. Peale and his executives went to Ottawa to make the proposal to the Government in more detail and that was the last that was heard of that.

A Canadian Automobile?

The management was well aware that it had often been proven impractical, if not impossible, to convert an aircraft organization into normal commercial work. Nevertheless, many avenues were explored, including that of the joint engineering and production, with an established auto maker, of a distinctly Canadian car. The concept was presented to George Romney and Roy Chapin, president and vice president respectively of American Motors in Detroit. At the time American Motors was not very active in Canada and considered the idea merit worthy and worth further investigation. A wholly Canadian company was envisaged which would apply the design, engineering, and manufacturing experience of American Motors, Avro and Orenda. In the course of the joint investigation, major changes in management at Malton took place and the proposed cooperative venture was not pursued.

The original concept of forming a basic Canadian company with a Canadian board of directors and management was, however, held valid by the Detroit executives. Without delay they appointed Earle Brownridge, until very recently president of Orenda, as chief executive officer of American Motors of Canada Ltd. A board of U.S. and Canadian executives was appointed. Mr. Brownridge purchased a farm near the town of Brampton and constructed a plant which was producing automobiles in less than a year.

At the official opening of the plant, Mr. Romney was to explain that his objective had been to have a truly Canadian company with Canadian investment participation. He said that he had gone to Toronto on more than one occasion in an endeavour to make this arrangement with the financial community with no success. He had been advised by the local financiers that they might give consideration to his proposal on the basis of five years experience of profitable operation. In any event he was happy to go it alone and did so successfully and very profitably from the outset. His dedication to Canada and serious concern over the direction of industrial policies of the Government led Mr. Brownridge to resign from the presidency of American Motors in order to run for parliament in the election of 1968. He won the Conservative nomination in his home constituency but was defeated in the election. His constituency was also that of a great number of ex Avro and Orenda employees who could not be expected to vote Conservative, even for Earle Brownridge. Mr. Brownridge died in 1973, at the age of 57.

6

WHY? THE CHAOS THAT FOLLOWED

Why?

Outlined below, is a breakdown of the final, total costs of the Arrow program in the amount of $404.2 million. Through the deliberate action of the Government nothing whatsoever was salvaged from this investment. In a parallel column is an estimate I have made of what it would have cost to complete the thirty-seven aircraft including spare parts, publications, and ground support equipment. My estimate is based on data which I have retained, my memory, and some educated guessing. In a recent appeal to the company (Hawker-Siddeley Canada), access to my old files was denied on the grounds that, "the company wants to maintain a low profile". It was assumed that the vital data required from Government files would be difficult to locate, if in fact it was still in existence. It is believed, however, that the figures are sufficiently accurate for their purpose.

	FEBRUARY 1959	TO COMPLETE
AVRO		
Development	67.7	87.7
Tooling	30.3	31.3
Production and Support	81.9	213.1
	179.9	332.1
ORENDA		
Development	55.4	71.9
Tooling	13.6	17.2
Production and Support	58.4	105.5
	127.4	194.6

J-75 & MISCELLANEOUS	9.6	9.6
TOTAL ARROW	316.9	536.3
Astra	34.0	34.0
Sparrow	27.0	27.0
Hughes MX-1179	1.7	11.7
	62.7	72.7
Total Program	379.6	609.0
Termination	24.6	----.--
Grand Total	404.2	609.0

BALANCE: $204.8

In other words, by spending roughly $200,000,000 the Government could have had thirty-seven airplanes with spares and equipment to maintain them. Surely these airplanes could have been put to a useful purpose in the defence of the country. Of equal importance, it would have bridged the gap until another project could have been undertaken. If there was to be no other project, it would have allowed the company time to wind down, and the employees to be gradually released in an orderly fashion.

Avro and Orenda were not normal commercial operations. They were defence contractors, solely, and had been throughout their existence. There can be no shadow of doubt as to the Government's responsibility for the two companies and their employees who served the Government and the country so well over nearly fifteen years.

Defence Expenditure Committee

In the spring of 1960, the Special Committee on Defence Expenditures reviewed the expenditures of the 1958-59 fiscal year. In so doing, the Arrow project was submitted to review and produced some revealing testimony, some of which is quoted in the paragraphs below.

Mr. Pearkes volunteered to make a brief statement to summarize the Arrow situation. He said, "The early concept (specification) for the replacement of the CF-100, which subsequently became known as the CF-105, or the Avro Arrow, was for an aircraft with a radius of 300 nautical miles, a combat ceiling of 60,000 feet and a maximum speed at high altitude of Mach 2." Here the Defence Minister is giving the authoritative, formal statement of the project and errs in the definition of the vital specification—by quite a margin. In fact, the early concept, or specification, was a supersonic radius of action of 200 nautical miles with a maneuverability of 2g at 50,000 feet, at a speed of 1.5m without loss of speed or altitude.

In reply to questions on the range of the aircraft Mr. Pearkes said, "The subsonic combat radius of action is 506 nautical miles .... That is 582 statute miles. The radius for ferrying, or for moving, would be 750 miles in non-combat state .... 750 nautical miles, which is 862 statute miles". Reference to the company's performance data, shown previously, will reveal serious discrepancies.

In reply to a question from Mr. Hellyer, Mr. Pearkes said, "As long as there is a bomber threat, manned interceptors would be required and a means of defeating the bomber threat".

In reply to a further question from Mr. Hellyer, Mr. Pearkes said, in part, "There are, however, important factors necessitating the continued use of manned interceptors in the air defence system for many years, indeed for as far as we can see into the future". He had apparently forgotten the PM's statement of a little over a year earlier, when the exact opposite was said and given as the prime reason for cancelling the Arrow.

Mr. Hellyer: But the PM gave the impression the company should have known cancellation was inevitable. Would you agree on that?
Mr. Pearkes: Yes I would.
Mr. Hellyer: Did you at any time between September and February tell the company that cancellation would be announced shortly?
Mr. Pearkes: No, because they were not told cancellation would be announced at any particular time.
Mr. Forgie: What advice did NORAD give to the Government prior to the cancellation of the Arrow contract?
Mr. Pearkes: I do not think I should answer this question.

A prominent article by Robert Crichton in the *Globe and Mail* of November 24, 1958, provided the answer to this question. It was written after a visit to NORAD headquarters and interviews with the Commander, General Partridge, and the Deputy Commander, Air Marshal Slemon. The prominent heading of the article was "Avro Arrow next to indispensable to NORAD, Air Marshal indicates". In the body of the article, it stated that the Commander agreed with his Deputy.

Mr. Hellyer: A number of senior military advisers made public statements to the effect that manned interceptors would be required as far ahead as they could determine--at least through the greater part of the 1960's. Statements along this line were made by General Partridge, Air Marshal Slemon, General Kuter, General Thomas White, Commander in Chief USAF, General Pearkes, General Taylor, General Twining and others .... Can the Minister give the Committee any public statement of any senior military person during the same period in which the contrary opinion was expressed?
Mr. Pearkes: No, I do not know of any serving officer of either the army or the air force who made a public statement to the contrary effect. That

is any Canadian serving officer, I cannot say anything about the American serving officers.

In dealing with costs--

Mr. Pearkes: Certainly the final estimates of the costs that were received were never contemplated in the early consideration that was given to this project. In fact, the costs had risen from an early estimate of $1.5 million to $2 million per plane, to $12.5 million per plane, if it had included the original fire control system: or $7,800,000 if the alternative or modified fire control system had been introduced. . . . All I can say in conclusion is that the cost of $12.5 million for an aircraft, or even, if the alternative system of fire control had been introduced, of $7,800,000 was just a price tag which was too high to be included in the defence budgets of those days.

On the surface and without explanation these figures are quite staggering and presumably deliberately put forth in this manner for a purpose. The $1.5 to $2 million figure was based on a quantity of five hundred to six hundred airplanes--complete operational airplanes only. It did not include design and development, tooling, spares, ground support equipment, missiles, etc. The other figures were achieved by basing the price of one hundred airplanes and then piling on top of it all the other costs. From the Minister's remarks, one would gain the impression that the reason for cancellation was economic, not strategic, as was originally advertised.

In a later part of the meeting, Mr. Hellyer asked: "What I would like to ask the Minister to provide, if he would do so, in order that we might have the information, is the breakdown of the difference between that 3.45 and the totals he gave us on a per copy basis if we had gone into volume production and had it available for sale over and beyond our own requirement."

Then Mr. Miller (Deputy Minister) responded:

I might answer this question. . . . The offer of the company was $3,750,000 per copy. Now the term they use to associate with that is 'fly away'. That is, if they were allowed to produce one hundred airplanes, they would sell all those airplanes as a bare airplane, for that amount of money. So if, on the face of it, you took one hundred of them, you would multiply that figure by one hundred. What they did not include in that, was the continuation of the development of the airplane to the point where it could be put into production as a fully free operational airplane. That figure was $295,000,000. This was the estimate made at the time. If you add it up, that automatically adds another $3,000,000 to the price. This was a continuing development of that aircraft from configuration, which they were quoting on at that time. That was estimated to be the amount. In addition, you had to have the spare support and ground handling equipment, which was of the order of $100,000,000. Then the procurement of the necessary weapons adds another $50,000,000. So the figure to which the Minister has referred, in the amount of 7.8 million dollars per copy is the average cost of the 100 airplanes, starting at the basic cost of $3,750,000. And working it up, with all the attendant factors, it comes out to this figure. That would be for the first one hundred copies, on the basis of your figures, at volume production, if proceeded with.

The only item missing in this price calculation was the pay and allowances of the airforce.

Firstly, Mr. Miller's basic price of $3,750,000 is incorrect and should have been $3,500,000. Nevertheless, on the basis of his figures the total per plane should have been $8,200,000, and then by deleting the cost of the missiles, the total becomes $7,700,000. To reach an average unit cost, however, the total should have been divided by 137 which would have resulted in a unit cost of $5,620,000. The thirty-seven airplanes were contained in Mr. Miller's figure of $295,000,000 which was added to the basic price. In other words, the thirty-seven airplanes were written off as a development expense.

Even in the original concept of the project, some of the thirty-seven airplanes were considered to be operational. With the elimination of the Astra and the Sparrow, fewer development airplanes would have been required. With the supposition that only one hundred operational airplanes were required, the whole development program could have been adjusted to reflect further savings had there been any consultation with the company. In the case of the product airplanes, the company could and did, with considerable risk, act on its own. This was not possible in the case of the development program but no one in the Government seemed interested at the time.

As the Government did not take the company into its confidence, the company was asked to make estimates in the dark. For example, it is one thing to plan a development program for a long term production run of some hundreds of airplanes and something else for a production run of one hundred. Obviously, a development project such as the Arrow, would never be undertaken for one hundred operational airplanes, however, in the case of the Arrow, when the number required was, rightly or wrongly, reduced to one hundred, a greater part of the development had been completed at a cost of some $400,000,000.

In defence projects such as that of the Arrow, it is imperative that there be the closest possible relationship and cooperation between Government agencies and the contractor, lack of which has been illustrated by the Arrow fiasco. In the case of the Arrow project, it was not merely a lack of cooperation but, rather, that the appropriate Government officers were forbidden, under dire consequences, to disclose the thinking or plans of the Government to the company.

It was estimated that the cost of the second one hundred operational airplanes would have been $2,600,000 and, in this case, the costs of development and tooling could not be added as they would have been absorbed in the $5,620,000 price.

In his report to the House of Commons the chairman of the Committee was to write,

> Your Committee noted that the bomber threat against the North American continent is substantial and the expectation that, during the next few years, it would continue to be so, although diminishing in scale. Provision has been made in the estimates to improve the defences against this threat through a joint programme with the United States providing the Bomarc surface-to-air missile, strengthening and adding to the Pine Tree radar control system and providing SAGE electronic control and computing equipment. In view of the opinion expressed by the Minister that the period of effectiveness of the CF-100 is limited, the Committee hopes that an early decision can be taken as to the advisability of obtaining a replacement for this aircraft.

At a much later date, the internal gyrations of the Government and the military were revealed in an unpublished summary of the Arrow project written by the late General Foulkes. He wrote, "Much has been said but not much revealed." He then proceeded, in essence, to reveal the following,

> Upon the Government's return to office in March 1958, it was apparent that outstanding defence matters must be settled, particularly the future of the Arrow. Accordingly, the Joint Chiefs of Staff Committee undertook a study of the various factors involved. The Defence Production Department advised that approximately $300,000,000 had been spent on the Arrow project and that an additional $871,000,000 would be required to complete it. This resulted in the $12,500,000 figure. This would not leave much for other requirements in a diminishing defence budget.

> The alternative was to cancel the Arrow project in its entirety and to negotiate with the U.S. Government to acquire two Bomarc stations, with the necessary SAGE equipment and one hundred interceptors, at an estimated price of about $2,000,000 each.

> Apparently these two courses of action with the emphasis on the second, over the objection of the Chief of Air Staff, were placed before the Minister of Defence. The Minister, in turn, recommended the cancellation of the Arrow and the acquisition of the Bomarc, SAGE and interceptors from the U.S.

It is obvious that, in the above deliberations, economics was the major consideration of the military Committee.

It would seem that, about this time, the company provided the input of the Hughes fire control system and missile, and out of these conflicting considerations the Governments choice was as outlined in the statement of September 23, 1958. It is not known if the decision to cancel the Arrow was taken then, but events were certainly moving in that direction. It is surmised that it was decided to take the first bite at it by cancelling the Astra and Sparrow and then to assess public reaction, particularly with regard to the Arrow, a trial balloon so to speak. The Christmas recess of the House was coming up and the MP's could assess the reaction in their constituencies.

General Foulkes continues,

> In the latter part of 1958, the Chiefs of Staff were asked again to submit a proposal to the Government. Apparently, the PM indicated that he would not entertain a proposal that involved the cancellation of the Arrow with the procurement of a U.S. substitute. Accordingly, a submission was prepared to provide for the cancellation of the Arrow leaving for further study the matter of the interceptor replacement. The Chief of the Air Staff refused to go along with this decision. In order to cover up dissention amongst the Chiefs of Staff, the Minister decided to put forth the submission without any recommendation from the Chiefs of Staff.

Air Marshal Campbell could not and did not go along with the proposal on the grounds that it would leave the country wide open to any supersonic bomber attack. It is difficult to understand how the other Chiefs of Staff could subscribe to this proposal, having a full knowledge of these facts. In the case of the cancellation statement of February 20, 1959, it was not only that the PM did not act on the advice of the military experts, but that he acted against the advice of the primary authority and the officer responsible for the air defence of Canada, the CAS of the RCAF. Neither the CAS of the RCAF nor the chairman of the Joint Chiefs resigned, however, therefore condoning the situation and giving substance to the PM's statement.

The net result of the foregoing may be summarized as follows. The air defence of Canada was to be based upon nine squadrons of subsonic CF-100s and two stations of untried Bomarc B missiles, which are only effective with the installation of nuclear warheads. The primary requirement of these missiles was for the protection of SAC bases in the U.S. As a by-product they were to provide some protection for the Toronto and Montreal areas. Whereas the missile was at best considered a supplementary weapon to the interceptor as the last defence against bombers that have infiltrated the interceptors, it was now Canada's only defence.

The technical organizations at Malton had been deliberately destroyed and the facilities abandoned thus, once again, making the RCAF completely dependent on equipment from the U.S. The Canadian industry had been relegated to the role of subcontractor to the U.S. industry. The Arrows and Iroquois, together with the advanced technology which they reflected, were scrapped. The first step was taken for the dissolution of the operational arm of the RCAF. These actions and events, all wrong and unnecessary, will no doubt be recorded as one of the worst military and industrial disasters of

Canadian history.

The Bomarc

The Bomarc was a product of Boeing Aircraft Company in Seattle. The Bomarc B, chosen by the Government, was an outgrowth of the Bomarc A. It was to be powered with solid fuel and armed with a nuclear warhead. The program for its development started early in 1958.

In 1959 the Bomarc project became embroiled in an inter-service dispute with the Army's Nike-Hercules missile. As a result, appropriations for both projects were reduced. Furthermore, the first test of the Bomarc B in May 1959 was a failure as were several successive ones. In March 1960, the USAF accelerated its interceptor projects and further cut the Bomarc program, which was now in jeopardy. The funds for the project were reduced to a relative token and the planned number of installations reduced to eight, plus two in Canada. Observations were made from several quarters that the USAF would have scrapped the program completely had it not been for the commitment to Canada. Later, and with the full knowledge of its effect on Canada, the U.S. Appropriations Committee recommended the scrapping of the project.

This, of course, placed the Canadian Government in an impossible position. It endeavoured to deny the press reports coming from Washington and emphasized its confidence in the Bomarc, without foundation, as the missile was yet to be successfully tested. The position was that the USAF was keeping alive the development of a weapon, which it considered unacceptable, for the sole purpose of making it available to Canada.

As a result of pressure by the Canadian Government and the first successful firing of the missile in the spring of 1960, the fate of the Bomarc turned around. Some of the funds were restored to the project, which continued with limited success.

As debate in the House raged over the status of the Bomarc in the US, finally, the Liberal Opposition put forward some views of its own. It declared its opposition to the use of nuclear weapons and accordingly to the Bomarc. It pointed out all of the obvious defects of the Bomarc as a weapon for the defence of Canada and proposed the use of interceptors instead, if only for the purpose of identification.

The two Bomarc stations were completed in the fall of 1961 and would have become operational in the spring of 1962 except that the missiles had no warheads and as a consequence were useless. The agreement with the U.S. Government for the handling and control of the nuclear warheads was still being debated. The fact was that the Canadian Government was stalling over the whole nuclear situation and continued to do so throughout its term in office rendering the Bomarcs useless for the same period. Canada, therefore, was defenceless against a supersonic bomber attack. It was not until 1964 that the nuclear problem was partially resolved when Canada had at least some pretence of defence. In February 1963 the U.S. Defence Secretary, Robert McNamara, declared before a Congressional sub-committee that the Bomarc was useless. In 1971 the Trudeau Government decided to dismantle the Bomarc stations.

In the concluding paragraph of Chapter 2, Volume 3 of his memoirs, Mr. Diefenbaker was to summarize this sad episode.

> Our decision to introduce the Bomarc did not work out well. To begin with, the Bomarc was very soon proven to be virtually obsolete, even before it was set up. The day of the bomber was over. The Bomarc was ineffective against Intercontinental Ballistic Missiles. Further, no information was given U.S. that the United States would abandon, or had abandoned, its plans to manufacture a conventional warhead for their missile. Had I even an inkling of what was to come, there would have been no announcement on September 23, 1958, of our decision to introduce the Bomarc, because no such decision would have been taken.

F-104

As indicated previously, the unalterable policy of the Liberal Government since World War II was that the role of the RCAF would be purely defensive. Apparently, in the midst of consideration of the Arrow project, the Government knowingly or otherwise agreed to convert the role of the RCAF Air Division in NATO from defensive with CF-100s and F-86s to a strike attack role utilizing the F-104 armed with nuclear weapons.

Also, as indicated previously the strike attack aircraft of the USAF was the Republic F-105, a big, heavily armed airplane. The F-104 was originally designed as a relatively light weight interceptor but lost out in the design competition with others. Lockheed Aircraft then proposed that the aircraft could be redesigned to fill the role of a relatively cheap strike attack airplane for sale to less fortunate allies. One of the first, if not the first, to swallow this bait was Canada. Shortly after the Arrow cancellation, Avro and Canadair were asked to submit proposals for the production of two hundred F-104s. Canadair was awarded the contract for the airplane and Orenda was awarded the contract to produce the General Electric J-79 engine in August 1959.

The first aircraft was produced in March 1961. Peak production was planned at fifteen per month. In addition to the two hundred airplanes for the RCAF, the U.S. Government bought an additional one hundred and forty for distribution to NATO countries. The airplane remained in production until August 1965.

The sole *raison d'etre* for the F-104 was as a carrier of nuclear weapons in a strike offensive role. Without weapons, of course, the airplane was useless—which it was until 1964. With a host of political implications, the RCAF role in Europe had been converted from a defensive to offensive one—but one without weapons. The situation at this point in the early sixties was that Canada's own sophisticated air defence weapon and the technical organizations which created it had been destroyed. The substitute missiles were reposing in their fixed installations unarmed and the attack weapon was flying around Europe, again unarmed. Within a short period of two years, the once mighty air force had been rendered useless.

F-101B

The McDonnell F-101B was a twin engine, two-man interceptor somewhat similar to the Arrow but not nearly as advanced in its design. Its armament originally consisted of the Hughes fire control system and the Falcon missile. Its subsequent armament was upgraded to the Geni nuclear missile, but not in Canada until 1964.

In June 1961, when the Arrow-Bomarc controversy had subsided, the Government announced that arrangements had been made to acquire sixty-six F-101Bs from the U.S. Government. This was not a normal purchase of aircraft from a U.S. manufacturer, but an inter-government arrangement which provided for the transfer of the aircraft from USAF stocks, in exchange for Canada taking over U.S. obligations in Canada such as the U.S. operated stations in the Pinetree Line. At long last the RCAF was to be provided with a supersonic interceptor although the quantity had dropped to sixty-six and, after all, ended up with the Hughes system and missile.

The McDonnell-Douglas successor to the F-101B was the F-4 Phantom, an aircraft more comparable with the Arrow. The following is quoted from an article in *Fortune* magazine of December, 1972.

> In the past fourteen years McDonnell-Douglas has built over 4,200 F-4s in eleven different versions. The latest version, the F-4E has a dash speed past Mach 2, a ferry range of about 1,800 miles, a combat radius of better than 450 miles, and is more expensive, $3,750,000.

That was the fly away price. The article went on to say that, in 1955-64, the average cost of the F-4 was $2,000,000 plus $825,000 to amortize development expense which, if applied to the 4,200 aircraft, works out to a little below $3.5 billion. This does not include the development cost of the engine or the fire control system. It is impossible to compare aircraft performance in general terms. It can only be done accurately to a common specification, including maneuverability, armament, and so forth. Even a superficial comparison of the F-4 in the early seventies, however, with the Arrow of the early sixties is revealing. The most revelatory statistic is the quantity produced, 4,200 airplanes, most of them with performance inferior to that of the Arrow. Further, this interceptor was in great demand close to fifteen years after the Diefenbaker statement of September 23, 1958.

Nuclear Armament and the Cuban Missile Crisis

When the decisions were made to acquire the Bomarc and the F-104, it automatically followed that nuclear armament would be used. The PM referred to this fact and said an agreement to provide for the acquisition of nuclear armament would be entered into with the U.S. At the time there was no serious contention with this situation.

In March 1959, the Minister of External Affairs, Sidney Smith, died. He was succeeded by the former Minister of Public Works, Howard Green. It would appear that shortly after this appointment, the attitude of the Government began to change. Mr. Green was vigorously opposed to nuclear armament and wished to become the leading advocate for worldwide disarmament. It would be inconsistent for Canada to adopt nuclear weapons joining the nuclear club and at the same time to become the champion of disarmament. Mr. Green was not alone in his views as, between 1960-62, the subject became a major item of debate not only in Canada but world-wide.

Throughout this period the Government stalled in its acquisition of armament for the Bomarc and F-104 and continued to make the usual ambiguous and misleading statements to cover up its indecision. It also refused permission to allow the USAF squadrons of interceptors, stationed at Goose Bay and Newfoundland, to use nuclear armament.

The Canadian debate also stormed around the question of control and storage of the weapons and the authority for their use. One view was that if they were acquired they must be under the control of the Canadian Government, but this was not possible owing to U.S. legislation. This in turn presented a situation whereby Canadian defence was in the hands of the U.S. These difficulties presented opportunities for manipulation and manoeuvre by Mr. Diefenbaker.

In this nuclear debate, conflicting statements by Mr. Pearkes in favour of nuclear weapons and by Mr. Green against, revealed a vast difference of opinion within the cabinet. Whether or not this was a factor, Mr. Pearkes retired in October 1960, apparently leaving the field to Mr. Green. Mr. Pearkes was replaced by Douglas Harkness. Early on it appeared that Mr. Harkness was a pro-nuclear man. This is not surprising since the two major weapons for which he was responsible were otherwise useless.

The Opposition Liberal Party did not contribute a great deal to the debate. They could see that public opinion appeared to be divided and they had previously indicated that they were, in principle, against the use of nuclear weapons. They were mainly concerned with unravelling the conflicting Government statements in order to ascertain its intention.

Even the campaign for the election of June 1962 failed to harden this issue. The position of the Government remained undefined in spite of the fact that the two carriers, the Bomarc and the F-104, were to enter service. The theory was that the nuclear weapons could and would be readily available in an emergency, which was not the case as an agreement had still to be entered into with the U.S. Government. Furthermore, considerable lead time was involved in the physical application of the weapons. Owing to their general performance, indecisiveness, muddled defence policy and financial mismanagement, the Conservatives lost their majority in Parliament in the election in June.

On October 22, 1962, President Kennedy informed the world of the magnitude of the crisis resulting from detection of Soviet missiles in Cuba. Prior to the President's speech, U.S. forces had been put on alert. The Canadian Government was advised of the situation beforehand, as well. This crisis was one of the most serious since World War II and one with an immediate direct bearing on Canada.

There is speculation as to the actions of the Canadian Government at this time of crisis but some vital points are clear: 1. that the cabinet did not order an alert until October 24; and 2. that although the Minister of Defence stated in the House on October 23 that no alert had been given he did, in fact, place the RCAF squadrons in NORAD on alert that day.

It is understood that the U.S. requested permission to arm their squadrons at Goose Bay and Newfoundland with nuclear missiles and to move some of their nuclear armed interceptors from their U.S. bases into Canada. This permission was denied. Mr. Diefenbaker admitted that some delay had been involved but endeavoured to defend it on grounds that Canada had not been fully consulted, as provided in the NORAD agreement. In any event, because of his previous actions Canada's military contribution was virtually meaningless. This impossible performance not only brought disgrace upon Canada but again brought to the fore the whole defence question, including the nuclear situation. The Government was sitting on the fence while the F-104 and the Bomarc remained unarmed.

The situation assumed similar proportions to the Arrow crisis. In the face of reality, as demonstrated by the Cuban crisis, the Liberal Party changed its position. USAF Generals were publicly commenting on Canada not fulfilling defence commitments. In January 1963 the Liberal Leader, Mr. Pearson, made a forceful statement in favour of nuclear weapons on the grounds that Canada must fulfil its commitments.

In response to the pressure, the PM made a typical and long statement in the House on January 25, 1963. He did not say the carriers would be armed with nuclear weapons but implied that discussions would again be held with the U.S. so that provision might be made for their acquisition in the case of emergency. On the basis of recent U.S. and British discussions, he even called into question the need for the F-104 strike force in Europe. The statement was yet another display of indecision and procrastination, on grounds that were completely fallacious.

As the PM's statement could be understood only by himself, the Defence Minister, Mr. Harkness, called a press conference to elaborate upon it, but in so doing partially contradicted it. Among other things he said it was definite policy to acquire nuclear arms. The PM repudiated the Defence Minister's remarks by saying that his speech was quite clear and needed no interpretation, whereupon the Opposition called for Mr. Harkness' resignation.

This statement and the whole defence situation had degenerated to such a serious although ridiculous level that the U.S. State Department felt called upon to make its own statement on Mr. Diefenbaker's speech on January 30. The U.S. statement repudiated very nearly all the PM had said, certainly, the tenor of his remarks.

> The Canadian Government has not as yet proposed any arrangement sufficiently practical to contribute effectively to North American defence. . . . The Soviet bomber fleet will remain at least throughout this decade a significant element in the Soviet strike force. An effective continental defence against this common threat is necessary.

The making of a public statement of this nature was unprecedented. Presumably it was made out of sheer exasperation and, after all, the subject of the PM's statement involved NATO and NORAD as well as the U.S. Government. On the basis of past experience, it would be reasonable to assume that the U.S. Government had given up any attempt to deal with the Government of Canada through normal channels. The action of the U.S., however, was viewed by all the Canadian political parties as unwarranted interference in Canadian affairs.

The following day, over the vigorous protests of the Government, the Opposition gained a motion to adjourn the House in order to discuss the U.S. statement and defence matters. It was obvious, during that session, that there was a wide division in the Government ranks.

On February 4, 1963, the Minister of Defence resigned in a public letter to Mr. Diefenbaker:

> For over two years you have been aware that I believed nuclear warheads should be supplied to the four weapons systems we have acquired which are adaptable to their use. It has become quite obvious during the last few days that your views and mine as to the course we should pursue for the acquisition of nuclear weapons for our armed forces are not capable of reconciliation.

This was the beginning of the end.

In the afternoon of the same day, Mr. Pearson made a motion of no confidence in the Government. As the Social Credit party had agreed to join the Liberals, the Government was defeated in the vote which took place on the evening of February 5, 1963. This dissolved Parliament. In the midst of the hubbub which followed, the acting Minister of Defence, Pierre Sevigney, and the Minister of Trade and Commerce, George Hees, also resigned, thus putting the finishing touch to the demise of the Diefenbaker Government. Diefenbaker had held out to the end along with his colleague Mr. Green, to ensure that the Bomarcs and the F-104s would remain unarmed.

Liberal Government Elected

As a result of the election of April 8, 1963, the Liberal Party formed another minority Government under the leadership of Lester B. Pearson. In May, Mr. Pearson stated his intention to make arrangements immediately with the U.S. Government for the acquisition of nuclear weapons to enable Canada, at last, to carry out her defence commitments. In August, he announced that these arrangements had been made (after five years of delay) providing for the joint control system in operation by the other NATO countries. In the spring of 1964, the F-101s, F-104s, and the Bomarcs received their nuclear capability, two years after the carriers were in place.

The critical views on the Bomarc of Paul Hellyer, the new Defence Minister had not changed; however, he believed that Canada should make some pretence of air defence and, because the cost of retaining them was minimal, he decided to do so.

Having laid to rest the manufactured nuclear crisis, the new Government turned its attention to other areas of defence. One of its major decisions was to unify the forces and within this context to create a Mobile Command. As the title indicates, this Command was to be mobile, flexible, reasonably self-contained, and prepared to act in any part of the world it might be required. It was intended to be a force for peace keeping duties, an extension of the duties which Canada had previously performed in conjunction with the United Nations.

Air support for this Command led to a requirement of twenty-four C-130 Hercules transports acquired from the U.S. and one hundred and thirty five Northrop F-5 fighters to be produced by Canadair. The F-5 is a light weight, supersonic, general purpose fighter. It is a single seat, twin-engine airplane with the armament hung externally, except for the cannon.

The contract was placed with Canadair in September 1965. The first aircraft was produced in February 1968 and production was planned at a peak rate of ten per month. An additional one hundred and five were ordered for the Netherlands, thus bringing the total to two hundred and forty airplanes which were completed in July 1974. Unfortunately, as there was no application for the Canadian airplanes, the majority went from Canadair to an RCAF hangar for storage.

The transport requirement also involved the purchase of fifteen Buffalo aircraft from De Havilland. This was the second small purchase by the Canadian Government of the DeHavilland medium range, short take-off types. De Havilland's major support had come from the U.S. army.

The Pearson Government continued the downgrading of the Canadian air defence system and took no steps to replace the ageing F-101s. The original meagre sixty-six were diminishing by attrition. Similarly, the F-104s in NATO received low priority and were likewise being reduced.

The Aurora

The last Government aircraft procurement was for the F-5 in 1965. The Argus coastal patrol aircraft had been in service since the early fifties. It was a modified version of the Bristol Britannia of the post war era. In early 1972, the Trudeau Government decided that the ageing Argus should be replaced. Requests for proposals were sent to Hawker-Siddeley in the U.K. and to Lockheed and Boeing in the U.S. The document outlined a two phase contract. Phase one was for Concept Definition which was to be at the expense of the companies. Hawker-Siddeley's proposal was based on the Nimrod, Boeing's on a substantially modified 707, and Lockheed's on the Orion.

In December 1973, the Government announced that Boeing and Lockheed were chosen to receive the phase two contracts, the costs for which the Government would pay. The estimated costs, however, were too high and discussions were held with both contractors in order to bring them down to an acceptable level. In May 1974 phase two contracts were placed with Boeing and Lockheed.

In December 1975, Lockheed was announced as the winner. The next step was negotiation of the supply contract, which presented some difficulties, mainly concerning the method of financing the project. It may be recalled that Lockheed was experiencing considerable financial difficulties at the time. This in turn resulted in differences of opinion within the Cabinet which was recorded in substantial coverage in the press. This contract was the first to provide for substantial offset work to be placed in Canada.

Finally, in June 1976 the contract was awarded to Lockheed for eighteen modified Orions, renamed the Aurora. The price per complete aircraft was $38.7 million. With the inclusion of spare parts, support equipment, etc., the total package came to $1.03 billion or $57.2 million each. The first aircraft was due for delivery in May 1980. The offset package was to be of a value of $900 million of work to be placed in Canada between 1976 and 1994.

Approximately four years elapsed from the Government decision to buy an airplane until a purchase contract was awarded. It will be an additional four years before the first plane is delivered and, probably, a further two years before it could be considered to be in service. The Aurora is a big airplane, with four turbo-prop engines, not unlike the Argus in general appearance. Its advancement is reflected in the avionics and armament.

The New Fighter

As the RCAF was still operating a diminishing handful of F-101s and a relatively few F-104s, both of the mid-fifties vintage, the Trudeau Government was faced with the choice of completing the disbanding of the operational arm of the RCAF or of providing it with new equipment. In March 1977, the Minister of National Defence announced that a new fighter would be acquired within a program cost of $2.34 billion. Apparently it was decided that one type of aircraft could perform all future fighter roles of the airforce, one definite role being that of an interceptor for the air defence of Canada. Delivery of the first airplane was scheduled for 1981 and for squadron use in 1983.

Five types of aircraft were selected as being those most likely to meet the requirements, and their manufacturers were asked to submit proposals for various quantities of aircraft, complete with support equipment, up to a maximum of 150 aircraft. The proposals were also to outline offset programs for Canadian industrial participation. The following aircraft proposals were submitted:

> GRUMMAN AEROSPACE CORPORATION F-14. This airplane is two man twin-engine. It is the largest, heaviest and most complex of the competitors and accordingly the most expensive. Produced for the U.S. Navy, it has a variable geometry wing.
>
> MCDONNELL-DOUGLAS F-15. This airplane is single seat, twin-engine. It is described as an "Air Superiority Fighter", a general purpose airplane. With limitations, it can perform the interceptor role and with more severe limitations it could function in the strike attack role. It is in production for the USAF.
>
> GENERAL DYNAMICS CORPORATION F-16. This airplane is single seat, single-engine. It is the lightest and the least expensive. Again, it is a general purpose, air superiority fighter, mainly for use in daylight operations. It would have serious difficulties in fulfilling either of the present roles of the RCAF. It is being produced in greater quantities than the others, for the USAF and other NATO countries.

NORTHROP CORPORATION F-18L. This airplane is single seat, twin-engine. It has the general characteristics of the F-16. It is a land based and lighter version of the F-18A in production for the U.S. Navy. Although it is the latest type, it is in the development stage and may be too late to meet the requirements of the RCAF.

PANAVIA AIRCRAFT GmnH TORNADO. The company is a consortium of British and European constructors. The airplane is two man, twin-engine. Although the airplane is billed as a multi-role fighter, it is primarily a strike attack fighter with an all weather capability. It is a sturdy, complex airplane with a variable geometry wing and reputedly the second most expensive.

These airplanes are the next generation of fighters, reflecting the latest developments in materials, aerodynamics and, above all, avionics and weapons. The Arrow was likewise capable of substantial development and had the capacity to accommodate the complex avionics and weapons. This new breed of fighters can perform roles for which the Arrow was not designed, nevertheless, a developed Arrow could have met the current interceptor requirements. With only one airplane chosen in the current competition, Canada will compromise, to a degree, the two present roles of the RCAF. With the Arrow covering the interceptor role, the RCAF would have had a clear choice for the second role.

The prices and costs of the contending airplanes are not available but a distillation of various published educated guesses has been made in order to provide a rough comparison. The prices are in millions of dollars expressed in unit costs. The quantity in the number of aircraft which could be bought for $2.34 billion. The Arrow price includes amortization of development and tooling but does not reflect the cost of present day avionics.

	F-14	F-15	F-16	F-18L	Tornado	Arrow
Fly away price	18.85	14.70	10.40	12.60	13.00	4.60
Total program	26.00	21.00	14.00	18.00	21.00	n/a
Quantity	90.00	111.00	167.00	130.00	111.00	n/a

As previously indicated, airplane performance can only be compared and assessed against a common specification for a specific mission. Although performance data in the case of these airplanes is classified, the table which follows will provide some comparison of the basic characteristics of three of the aircraft compared with the Arrow 2A and the projected Arrow 3.

	F-14	F-15	F-16	Arrow 2A	Arrow 3
Weight, lbs	60,000	45,000	30,000	70,000	80,000
Length, feet	62	64	48	78	78

Wing, sq ft	565	608	300	1200	1200
Engines	2	2	1	2	2
Thrust, lbs	21,000	25,000	25,000	26,000	27,000
Combat Speed, M	2+	2+	2+	2+	3+
Altitude, feet	60,000	60,000	60,000	60,000	70,000+
Crew	2	2	1	2	2
Estimated $/lb	$314	$426	$347	$66	n/a

As in the case of the Aurora, these airplanes will be purchased outside of Canada. In order to finance the undertaking, great stress has been placed on the ability of the manufacturer to place offset purchases in Canada. It has been stated by Government officers that this aspect of the project is as important, if not more so, than the performance and/or the price of the airplane. Furthermore, the offset purchases are not limited to the defence industry but include the whole industrial spectrum.

Amongst the considerable publicity surrounding the purchase, I was astounded to read the financial column by Ronald Anderson in the Toronto *Globe and Mail* of March 2, 1978. It reads, in part,

> But the big Los Angeles aircraft company (Northrop) has added two more elements to its industrial benefits programme. One is an export expansion programme intended to help diverse Canadian manufacturers to find new markets abroad, while the second is a new venture programme designed to secure Canadian participation in advanced technology programmes in which Northrop is involved.
>
> In assessing the export potential of Canadian industry, Northrop has concluded that markets can be found for about one half of the categories of goods manufactured in Canada, principally in the Middle East and Asia. The company would not buy the products on its own account, nor would it arrange for the sale. Its function would be to bring Canadian producers and potential foreign buyers together.

Something is very wrong when an aircraft company in California proposes to lead an export sales drive for diverse Canadian manufacturers for an estimated amount of $2 billion worth of business. The U.S. company also appears a peculiar source for the development of Canadian advanced technology. The company apparently subscribes to the theory that Canada is a northern banana republic with a branch plant economy.

7

RETROSPECTIVE

The Avro Jetliner gave Canada the capability for world leadership in intercity air transportation by several years. This was lost by default. Initially, the problem stemmed from a lack of confidence in the capability of the fledgling young company by the president of TCA and the Government (Mr. Howe). The company produced the product, as specified, but the authorities did not know what to do about it. When the company found a U.S. airline which did grasp the immense potential represented by the Jetliner, it was too late. Owing to pressure created by the war in Korea, the young company had to concentrate all of its efforts into putting into production its two other technical successes, the CF-100 and the Orenda engine. In terms of dollars, technology and prestige, the Jetliner cancellation was an incalculable loss to Canada.

During the war and after, until the election of the Diefenbaker Government in 1957, there was the closest relationship and cooperation between the U.S. and Canada at the political, military, and industrial levels in matters of air defence and supply. The relationship of Canadian Ministers to their opposite numbers in the U.S. was on a first name basis, as was the case with many of the NATO partners. The key Canadian Ministers were highly respected for their ability and their accomplishments. In matters of defence they spoke from strength as represented by the RCAF and the technological capacity of its air industry.

In 1957 Canada had a thriving aircraft industry. Canadair was in full scale production of the Orenda powered F-86. The total of 1,815 were to be completed in little more than a year. The T-33 jet trainer was in parallel production with the F-86 at a rate in excess of one per day, under a contract for a total of 652 airplanes. The big Argus coastal patrol aircraft was also being produced.

DeHavilland was producing the Tracker for the Canadian Navy. It was also in various stages of production of the Beaver, Otter, and Caribou, primarily for the U.S. Army although some of the Otters were for the RCAF.

Avro was in full scale production of the CF-100 Mk4 and 5 at a rate of one per day. In June, the month of the election, the sale was announced of 53 CF-100s for use by the Belgian air force. Little over a year was to pass for the completion of production of 682 airplanes. Orenda was producing engines for the CF-100 and F-86 at a rate of 100 per month and its contracts for 3,838 Orendas were to be completed in eighteen months. Avro had been working for close to four years on the design, development, and manufacture of an advanced supersonic fighter for the RCAF which was to be unveiled in a few months. Orenda was test running the big engine that was to power it.

These three aircraft companies together with the engine company represented a strong and efficient industry employing some 30,000, highly skilled, people capable of meeting the needs of the RCAF.

The RCAF was completing the establishment of fifteen F-86 and CF-100 squadrons in Canada to operate under NORAD, in the process of being formed, as well as twelve squadrons of the same airplanes in the Air Division in Europe under NATO. The RCAF had a compliment of over 1,000 first line combat fighters and was ranked amongst the great airforces in the western world.

Within a little over a year after the election of his Government in June 1957 and as the last F-86s and CF-100s were being delivered to the RCAF, Mr. Diefenbaker announced that the new supersonic fighter, which had had its first flight six months previously, was obsolete and probably would not be required.

Four and a half years after this announcement, in February 1963, the Government of Mr. Diefenbaker was defeated. During his term in office, he and his Government had altered the situation to the scenario outlined below.

The vital close cooperation with the U.S. had degenerated into confrontation and mistrust. Relations with the U.S. had rarely been so poor resulting from the attitudes and actions of Mr. Diefenbaker and his Ministers of External Affairs. It could fairly be stated that their attitude was anti-American. It is difficult to imagine how a Canadian Government could discharge its solemn responsibility for the defence of the country and the joint defence of North America in such circumstances.

The air defence of Canada was dependent upon sixty-six partially obsolescent F-101s which in the U.S. had been superseded by the F-4. Although there were CF-100s and F-86s in service they had become obsolete as a defence against supersonic bombers. There were also the Bomarcs, useless as they were unarmed. The defensive squadrons of the

RCAF in Europe were being reduced and converted to the attack role with F-104s, but again they were inoperative as they were unarmed.

Canada's own supersonic fighter which could and should have been in service with the RCAF, with a performance exceeding all others, was on the scrap heap, together with its engine. The technical organizations and the technology which they represented had vanished–lost by Canada forever. What had been a great air force in 1957 had been reduced to impotency. The prestige Canada had earned over the years and the authoritative voice of her Ministers was no longer there.

The Diefenbaker Government had several choices and, in my opinion, it established an unenviable record of 100% error.

The first error was in the acquisition of the Bomarc, an unproven, anti-bomber, nuclear armed missile and to assume it to be the major element in Canada's air defence system. The missile was never intended for such a role but presumably the Government grasped at it, as it was relatively cheap (the U.S. paying most of the cost) and would provide the pretence that it was a major contribution to air defence in the missile age.

The second error was the decision to change the role of the RCAF in NATO from defence to attack. This established the requirement for a new aircraft and placed Canada in the role of a potential aggressor in Europe. Were other NATO members to perform the air defence role, so successfully carried out by the Air Division, the RCAF squadrons should have returned to Canada, thus also eliminating the need for a new airplane.

As a result of these two errors, the apparent total Canadian requirement for the Arrow was reduced to 100, which set the stage for the third and crucial error–the cancellation of the Arrow.

The Arrow was Canada's interceptor and there was no question of its requirement, performance or capability. Some three hundred were required to replace the CF-100 in Canada and a similar quantity should have been required to replace the F-86 and CF-100 in Europe. These airplanes should have been produced, notwithstanding the relatively high unit cost. At the date of cancellation, some $400 million had been invested in the project. The annual cost was within Canada's economic capacity. Once in production, there could be little doubt that substantial quantities would have been ordered, on the basis of past experience and the high performance of the airplane. It will be recalled that over 4,000 F-4s were produced and, in the same time scale, the Arrow was a more advanced airplane. What was also abandoned was the last vestige of independence of the RCAF, one of the goals established in 1945 arising out of bitter wartime experience.

Had the Arrow been in production and in service with the RCAF in 1965, it is conceivable that there would not have been a need for the F-5 although the primary roles of the two aircraft were different. Also, had the

Arrow been in service in 1977, it is conceivable that a new aircraft for operation in Canada would not have been required. Although the new breed of fighters can perform roles for which the Arrow was not designed, nevertheless, the developed Arrow could have met the current interceptor requirement.

This third error automatically involved the fourth, namely, the ruin of the two technical organizations and their facilities. This not only involved the Malton organization but hundreds of others who were carrying out various phases of advanced technology. This was not restricted to the aircraft industry. For any Government deliberately to destroy such a gigantic investment in technology and such a national asset, is beyond comprehension. It must reflect a lack of awareness or rejection of the importance of technology to the future of Canadian industry which Mr. Diefenbaker has confirmed in his memoirs. Such actions and policy result in Canadian manufacturing remaining in the wilderness.

The fifth error, if it could kindly be referred to as such, was the brutal outright termination of the contracts for the thirty-seven Arrows and their engines without prior consultation with the company. It was the Government's responsibility, in conjunction with the company, to determine the proper, humane, and responsible means of dealing with the airplanes and the engines, the technical staff, and the workers who had built them. These organizations had worked exclusively on behalf of the Government for fifteen years. There could have been reasonable solutions to these problems had they been approached by reasonable men.

The Government had apparently made two concurrent decisions. One was not to produce the Arrow thus concluding advanced aeronautical development. The other was to produce the F-104. Would it not have been logical for a responsible Government to so inform the company and ask for a proposal as to how this transition might be accomplished in the most economical fashion with the least amount of disruption!

Finally, the deliberate, wanton destruction of the flying airplanes, the completed engines, the engineering and technical data and records, films, photos, all of the technology reflected in the airplane and the engine and fifteen years of experience, could only be an act by a person or persons of unsound mind.

The errors of the Diefenbaker Government were of course laid on top of the first two basic errors, in the selection of the Astra system and Sparrow II missile, committed by the previous Liberal Government.

The best illustrations of the confusion and contradictions are to be found in Volume 3 of Mr. Diefenbaker's memoirs. Referring to his early days in office he wrote, in part, "We decided to continue the CF-105 program because it seemed the right thing to do, pending developments: *our air defence experts were impressed by its trials and recommended it* ." [The italics are mine.] The crux of his remarks are contained in the following two paragraphs:

> It came before the Cabinet Defence Committee on 21 August and before Cabinet on 28 August. My colleagues and I took particular note of that part of the air defence review which read: 'Finally the cost of the CF-105 programme as a whole is now of such magnitude that the Chiefs of Staff feel that to meet the modest requirements of manned aircraft presently considered advisable, it would be more economical to secure a fully developed interceptor of comparable performance in the United States.' By accepting a recommendation to abandon the Arrow and investigate other aircraft and missile possibilities, the Government would have a year to decide whether it would re-equip our air defence fighter force wholly with missiles or with an alternative aircraft or with a combination of both.
>
> We fully appreciated that abandoning the CF-105 would be a shock to the Canadian aircraft industry. We therefore decided to give A.V. Roe and Orenda Engines Ltd. what amounted to a six-month formal notice that they might adjust gradually to their new situation. On 23 September I announced that we would not proceed to production but would continue the development phase of the Arrow and Iroquois engine until March 1959, at which time we would make known our final decision. The Arrow's special flight and fire control system, Astra, and its weapon system, Sparrow were to be terminated immediately.

The foregoing would give the impression that the Government did formally decide to cancel the Arrow project on August 28, 1958. Mr. Diefenbaker claims to have given "formal notice" to the company in his statement of September 23, where he states that in March 1959 he would make known his final decision, but in his September 23, 1958 statement he said, "the situation would be reviewed again". If it was decided on August 28, 1958 to cancel the Arrow in March 1959, why did he not give "formal notice" to Mr. Gordon in his meeting of September 17, 1958?

If Mr. Diefenbaker "gave formal notice" to the companies in his September 23 statement to the effect that the contracts were to be cancelled in March, why adopt the Hughes fire control system and missile? In his memoirs he said that much work had been done on the new system and that it was found to be practical but how was this possible as the Government had failed to obtain security clearance for the company to visit Hughes Aircraft?

Further on in this chapter Mr. Diefenbaker wrote,

> The Government's financial experts calculated the cost of the CF-105 at $7.8 million each, including weapons, spare parts, and the completion of the development, but not including any of the $303 million spent prior to September 1958. This was too costly for Canada's defence budget. However, the issue was decided finally by the inability of the Chief of Staff to report any new military developments that would justify the Arrow's production. Thus, I announced to the House of Commons on 20 February

1959 the cancellation.

In his reference to the acquisition of the F-101, he wrote,

> In the meantime, we had been considering other steps to provide for our share of North American air defence. The need for a new interceptor had been on the books since the cancellation of the Arrow. This took on an added importance when the Bomarc system began to collapse. On 13 June 1960, General Pearkes wrote me in this regard.

This would appear to be at some variance with previous pronouncements and would confirm General Foulke's version of events.

The Diefenbaker memoirs continue,

> The Avro airframe and Orenda engine contracts should have been terminated at the same time as the others Astra and Sparrow. The extra six months failed to achieve our purpose to prevent a further wrench in an already sagging economy.

This is yet another reason for not cancelling the Arrow project in September 1958. It is that advanced by Messrs Barkway and Fraser in 1958 and probably the most accurate.

In his memoirs, with reference to the Arrow affair, Mr. Diefenbaker concentrates on the wholesale dismissal of the employees, the blame for which he endeavours to place on the company. This also became a major factor in the controversy at the time. The PM goes on at length to demonstrate that the companies knew that the contracts were to be cancelled on the strength of his ambiguous statement of September 23. In any event the matter was an irrelevant red herring as the companies were powerless to do anything of a practical nature, even if they had known. The dismissal of the employees was an automatic sequel to the abrupt termination of the contracts. Mr. Diefenbaker admits he was advised of this inescapable consequence in his meeting with Mr. Gordon. He presumably dismissed this advice as a hollow threat of political blackmail.

This is not the issue, however, rather, the conduct of his Government in regard to the air defence policy of Canada. I have endeavoured to establish that this conduct was primarily politically motivated, that it was critically wrong in every aspect, ruining the asset of advanced technology and rendering the country virtually defenceless against supersonic air attack.

On the 20th anniversary of the cancellation of the Arrow on February 20, 1979, the Hon George Hees was interviewed by the CBC. Extracts which follow will further illustrate the sheer incompetence of the Government.

> Okay, well it's a very simple story. The Arrow. I think the public will be interested in it, why it was never explained is inexplicable to me. . . . The main argument against the Arrow was that by the time we took over the Government in 1957, the Avro Arrow had become obsolete. Now, this plane was designed around 1952, for the previous Liberal Government, but

by 1957 and '58, it had become completely outdated for this reason - it was designed to fly up and intercept Russian bombers flying at a maximum altitude of 25,000 ft. And so the plane was designed with a fuel capacity and a missile capacity to fire into the Russian planes, that would get it up to 25,000 ft and allow the plane to return safely to its starting point. The trouble was that by 1957-58 when we took over, the Russians had developed a bomber that would fly at not 25,000 ft but 50,000 ft. And so of course, our interceptor, the Avro Arrow would have to fly 50,000 ft into the air, discharge its missiles into the Russian bomber, destroy the atomic bombs coming across at that time, and be able to return to earth. But with the design that had been put into the plane it would have not been possible for the plane to fly up and fly back. It would be able only to fly up to the 50,000 ft, then it would have expended all of its fuel and the plane would have of course crashed when it returned to earth to land. And that was of course not a practical idea at all, and so, instead of going ahead with the plan which would have cost the Canadian people three quarters of a billion dollars, because each plane cost seven million dollars to build, it was decided to scrap the whole plan because it was ridiculous to put seven hundred million dollars into a plan that was obsolete and produce a plane that simply wouldn't do the job, and couldn't do the job for which it had been originally designed, therefore would have been a complete waste of money to go ahead. . . . Well, the Bomarcs were perfectly sensible. The Bomarcs would do the job for which they were designed. The Arrow wouldn't do the job. As I've said to you earlier, no matter what combination of missiles or planes was used, the Avro Arrow was completely useless because the Russian bombers that would be coming over, and which these Arrows had been designed to intercept and destroy, simply could not be reached, or if they were reached, our plane would then crash on its return to earth, the plane would be destroyed and the pilot would be killed, and of course that was a completely impractical and impossible plan to carry out, so from the moment that we learned these facts about the Arrow, the Arrow was out. It would be a stupid thing to go ahead with the production of the Arrow because it had become a completely obsolete plane. . . . I've enjoyed talking to you very much, and I hope I've been able to clear up, or will be able to clear up when this is put on the air, something that has not been understood by the Canadian people I think ever since the unfortunate scrapping of the plane took place.

Apart from the provision of nuclear armament, the Pearson Government did nothing to strengthen Canada's air defence capability. Transport aircraft were acquired and F-5 fighters were produced by Canadair as components of the mobile force.

The first act of the Trudeau Government in the area of air defence was to dismantle the Bomarc stations in 1971. In 1972 the decision was made to replace the aging Argus. It was not until 1977 that it was decided to replace the F-101s and F-104s of the 1950s vintage. The new airplanes are scheduled for service in the early 1980s. In the meantime, and at this date,

Retrospective

Canada's contribution to the air defence of North America consists of a handful of obsolete F-101s. The acts of three successive Governments in the field of air defence over the past twenty ears must reflect a sad, almost pitiful, picture in the eyes of the world and particularly as far as our defence partner to the south is concerned.

What a different picture it might have been had the Canadian designed and produced Arrow and Iroquois been in service with the RCAF since 1961.

Twice within a decade, Canada stood on the threshold of world leadership in aviation technology and twice within a decade these unique opportunities were abandoned.

Thus, since 1945, the wheel has done a complete turn. In 1945 the RCAF was dependent on other governments for the supply of its equipment. By the mid-1950s the RCAF was reasonably independent and self-contained in so far as its vital fighters were concerned. But, twenty years later, the air force once more is back where it started, completely dependent on other governments and, yes, for an interceptor, declared obsolete twenty years ago.

VERSION HISTORY

When he died in 1985 Fred had not found a means to publish his typed manuscript. By 1989 I had privately printed and bound a limited run of both a hardcover and a cerlox softcover version which I presented to a few of Fred's close friends and family members and to the Canadian Aviation Museum in Ottawa. For many years I also maintained an internet HTML version on my own personal webspace. This 2014 version is an unedited copy of the original typed manuscript and is unchanged from the previous versions.

Randy Smye
Oakville, ON
2014